ENGLISH RELIGIOUS LIFE IN THE EIGHTH CENTURY

ENGLISH RELIGIOUS LIFE IN THE EIGHTH CENTURY

AS ILLUSTRATED BY CONTEMPORARY LETTERS

BY

THOMAS ALLISON, M.A.

SOMETIME SCHOLAR OF LINCOLN COLLEGE, AND VICE-PRINCIPAL
OF WYCLIFFE HALL, OXFORD; AUTHOR OF "LECTURES ON
ENGLISH CHURCH HISTORY (PRE-REFORMATION)"

GREENWOOD PRESS, PUBLISHERS
WESTPORT, CONNECTICUT

Originally published in 1929
by The Society for Promoting Christian Knowledge, London
and the Macmillan Company, New York

Reprinted from an original copy in the collections
of the Brooklyn Public Library

First Greenwood Reprinting 1970

Library of Congress Catalogue Card Number 75-106708

SBN 8371-3438-2

Printed in the United States of America

AD MEMORIAM

CAROLI PLUMMER

INTERPRETIS   PRAESTANTISSIMI

BAEDAE OPERUM HISTORICORUM

HOC OPUSCULUM

PREFACE

READERS of Erasmus's letters will get a wonderfully vivid picture of the age in which the writer lived. They will also get a wonderfully vivid picture of the writer himself, and of some of the persons with whom he corresponded. In a somewhat lesser degree, readers of eighth-century letters (written by Englishmen either at home or abroad) will have much the same experience. They will find the Papacy, in connection with missionary enterprise, depicted in a favourable light. They will get much information regarding Continental affairs. They will often get interesting sidelights on English affairs ; and, in particular, they will be enabled to supplement the somewhat meagre entries found in Symeon of Durham regarding political dissensions in Northumbria towards the end of the century.

It is, however, in the portraiture of individuals that these eighth-century letters have their greatest value. They show us the part played by religion in shaping individual lives. We are enabled to see something of the spiritual lives of saintly men—their inward struggles, the consolation which they derived from Holy

Scripture, the comfort brought to them by the consciousness that they were supported by their friends' prayers. Sometimes, as in the case of Boniface's long letter to Cuthbert, archbishop of Canterbury, a great height of spiritual experience is reached.

Not only do these letters enable us to gain a fuller understanding of such well-known men as Boniface and Alcuin ; but many a man, who otherwise would be little more than a name to us, becomes a living personality. For this reason—if for no other—a study of these letters is invaluable towards forming an estimate of contemporary religious life.

In the following pages an attempt is made, not so much to write an ecclesiastical history of England in the eighth century, as to paint a picture of personal religion at that period. The scope of the work is shown in the title. Attention is almost entirely confined to *subjects which are illustrated by contemporary letters*.

The general impression made by a study of these letters will probably be, that although there are very many dark spots in the picture of English religious life in the eighth century, yet the picture is by no means one of unrelieved gloom.

T. ALLISON.

ABINGDON, BERKS,
March 21, 1929.

CONTENTS

ABBREVIATIONS

A.O.B.	=Mabillon, *Annales Ordinis S. Benedicti.*
A.S.C.	=*Anglo-Saxon Chronicle.*
C.Q.R.	=*Church Quarterly Review.*
D.C.B.	=*Dictionary of Christian Biography.*
De Pontif. Ebor.	=Alcuin, *De Pontificibus et Sanctis Ecclesiae Eboracensis.*
De Sanctis Hagust.	=Aelred of Rievaux, *De Sanctis Ecclesiae Haugustaldensis.*
E.H.S.	=English Historical Society.
G.P.	=William of Malmesbury, *Gesta Pontificum.* R.S.
G.R.	=William of Malmesbury, *Gesta Regum.* R.S.
H.A.A.	=Anonymous *Historia Abbatum.*
H.A.B.	=Bede, *Historia Abbatum.*
H. & S.	=Haddan and Stubbs, *Councils and Ecclesiastical Documents.*
H.E.	=Bede, *Historia Ecclesiastica Gentis Anglorum.*
Hist. Hagust.	=Prior Richard's History of the Church of Hexham [*ap.* Raine, *Hexham*].
J.T.S.	=*Journal of Theological Studies.*
K.C.D.	=Kemble, *Codex Diplomaticus.*
Migne, *P.L.*	=Migne, *Patrologia Latina.*
Mon. Alc.	=Monumenta Alcuiniana, ed. Wattenbach and Dümmler.

ABBREVIATIONS

Mon. Mog.	=Monumenta Moguntina, ed. Jaffé.
Raine, *H.Y.*	=Raine, *Historians of the Church of York and its Archbishops.* R.S.
Raine, *Hexham*	=Raine, *Priory of Hexham.* Surtees Soc.
R.S.	=Rolls Series.
S.D.	=Symeon of Durham. Surtees Soc.
Vita Alch.	=Anonymous *Vita Alchuini.*
Vita Bonf.	=Willibald, *Vita S. Bonifatii.*
Vita Cutb.	=Bede's prose *Vita S. Cuthberti.*

CHRONOLOGICAL TABLE [1]

[1] This Table does not aim at completeness, being mainly confined to incidents mentioned in the succeeding chapters. It is largely based upon the *Continuatio* appended to Bede's *Historia Ecclesiastica*, and upon Symeon of Durham's *Historia Regum*. For Tables exhibiting the episcopal succession, see Stubbs, *Reg. Sac. Angl.*

A.D.

718. Second mission of Boniface to Frisia.

719. Death of Rathbod.

721. Daniel, bishop of Winchester, visits Rome.

„ Death of John of Beverley (bishop of Hexham and afterwards of York).

722. Pope Gregory II. makes Boniface a bishop.

726 × 727. Death of Tobias, bishop of Rochester.

729. Ceolwulf becomes king of Northumbria.

731. Acca expelled from Hexham.[1]

„ Bede's *Historia Ecclesiastica* completed.

„ Death of Brihtwald, archbishop of Canterbury, and succession of Tatwin.

732. Egbert made *bishop* of York.

733. Bede's visit to Egbert at York.

734. Bede's *Epistola ad Ecgbertum.*

735. Egbert made *archbishop* of York.

„ Nothelm made archbishop of Canterbury.

„ Deaths of Bede and of Pecthelm (bishop of Whithern).

737. Ceolwulf becomes a monk at Lindisfarne. Eadbert becomes king of Northumbria.

„ Death of Aldwine, bishop of Lichfield.

„ Forthere, bishop of Sherborne, visits Rome.

738 × 739. Death of Willibrord.

740. Cuthbert made archbishop of Canterbury.

„ Ethelbald, king of Mercia, invades Northumbria while Eadbert was engaged in Pictish war.

741. Death of Charles Martel. Succession of Carloman and Pippin (father of Charles the Great).

744. Resignation of Daniel, bishop of Winchester.

---

[1] Authorities differ as to the date. The year given is that which we find in the *Continuatio.*

A.D.

747. Council of Clovesho.

749. Ethelbald, king of Mercia, publishes charter of ecclesiastical and monastic liberty.

„ Death of Elfwald, king of the East-Angles.

751. Lullus visits Rome on embassy from Boniface.

754. Martyrdom of Boniface.

757. Ethelbald, king of Mercia, slain. Succession of Beornred, then of Offa.

758. Eadbert, king of Northumbria, becomes a monk.

759. Bregwin made archbishop of Canterbury.

765. Alhred (Alcred) becomes king of Northumbria

766. Jaenbert made archbishop of Canterbury.

„ Death of Egbert, archbishop of York.

768. Alhred marries Osgeofu (Osgearn).

774. Ethelred becomes king of Northumbria on flight of Alhred.

778. Resignation of Albert, archbishop of York. Succession of Eanbald I.

779. Expulsion of Ethelred. Accession of Elfwald.

781. Alcuin's meeting with Charles the Great at Parma.

786. Legatine mission of George and Theophylact.

„ Death of Lullus.

„ Cynewulf, king of the West-Saxons, slain.

787. Nicene Council (Image worship).

„ Lichfield made an archiepiscopal see. (Abolished in A.D. 802.)

788. Elfwald slain.

790. Ethelred restored.

791. Ethelheard made archbishop of Canterbury.

792. Ethelred marries Elfleda, daughter of Offa.

793. Lindisfarne plundered by the Northmen.

A.D.

794. Jarrow plundered by the Northmen.

„   Council of Frankfort.

„   Death of Pope Adrian I.

795. Charles the Great's victory over the Huns. His generosity to the Church and to the poor.

796. Deaths of Offa and of Egferth (king of Mercia for 141 days). Cenwulf succeeds.

„   Ethelred slain. Osbald king of Northumbria for 27 days. Eardulf succeeds.

„   Death of Eanbald I. Eanbald II. succeeds.

„   Alcuin made abbot of S. Martin, Tours.

796 × 797. Ethelheard flees from Canterbury.

797. Death of Ethelbert, bishop of Hexham.

798. Eadbert Praen, king of Kent, captured by Cenwulf.

798 × 799. Council of Pincanhalh.

799. Pope Leo III. maltreated.

800. Alcuin's disputation with Felix on Adoptionism.

„   Death of Queen Liudgarda.

„   Charles the Great crowned on Christmas Day in S. Peter's, Rome. His protection is invoked for the Christians in Jerusalem.

ENGLISH RELIGIOUS LIFE
IN THE EIGHTH CENTURY

CHAPTER I

THE POLITICAL SITUATION

NORTHUMBRIA

THE tragedy of Nechtansmere, where King Egfrid fought against the Picts and was slain, is regarded by Bede as marking a turning-point in the glory of the Northumbrian kingdom.[1] The decline was, to some extent, averted by his successor, the learned Aldfrid, who "nobly recovered the destroyed state of the kingdom, although within narrower limits."[2] On the death of that king (A.D. 705), we enter upon a period of gloom. The miserable tale of conspiracy, treachery, and bloodshed which we find in the *Anglo-Saxon Chronicle* and in Symeon of Durham's *Historia Regum* may be amplified, from time to time, by passages from contemporary letters. Aldfrid's son, the youthful Osred, succeeded to the throne after a brief period of usurpation on the part of a rival. The new king proved himself to be thoroughly debauched in cha-

[1] H.E. iv. 26.   [2] *Ibid.* l.c. Cf. G.R. i. 57–58.

racter. We have a famous admonitory letter addressed by Boniface and several other bishops to Ethelbald, king of Mercia.[1] The evil deeds of Ceolred—a king of Mercia to whom reference will be made later[2]— and of Osred are set forth, emphasis being laid on their violation of nuns. These two sinners, according to the writers, were " condemned by the just judgment of God, cast down from the royal height of this life, cut off by an untimely and terrible death, shut out from the everlasting light, and sunk in the deep abyss of hell." The writers add that a spirit of wantonness drove Osred to commit fornication with nuns, " until he lost his glorious kingdom, his youthful life, and his wanton soul by a contemptible and vile death."[3]

Of a later king, Ceolwulf, we have a more favourable account.[4] It is to him that Bede dedicates his *Ecclesiastical History*, speaking of the attention which the king paid to Holy Scripture, and of the interest which he took in history, especially in that of his own people. It is to him that a high tribute is paid in the *Epistle to Egbert*. The king's zeal for religion is mentioned, and Bede believes that he will prove a ready helper in Egbert's efforts to promote measures for the good of the Church.[5] But he had a troubled reign.[6] Ultimately

[1] Mon. Mog. pp. 168–177 ; H. & S. iii. 350–356.
[2] V. inf. pp. 10–11.
[3] Cf. H.E. v. 24 ; G.R. i. 58.
[4] William of Malmesbury well says (G.R. i. 58), " conscendit tremulum regni culmen."
[5] Ep. ad Egb. § 9.　　　　　[6] H.E. v. 23.

he resigned his kingdom and became a monk at Lindisfarne.[1]

In the course of the century, a legatine mission was sent by Pope Adrian I. to England.[2] The legates, George and Theophylact, held two Councils, one in Northumbria, the other in Mercia. They wrote a most interesting letter regarding their mission, informing the Pope of decrees which had been accepted for the furtherance of religion.[3] One of these decrees (No. 12) dealt with the election of kings and the honour due to the kingly office. Strong language is used with regard to the slaying of " the Lord's anointed." Any bishop or priest guilty of such a sin was to be deprived of office. Any person whatever who assented to such an act of sacrilege " would perish under an eternal bond of anathema, joined to Judas the traitor, and burn in everlasting fires." A striking commentary on the disregard in which these principles were often held throughout the century is furnished by the frequency with which kings of Northumbria met with violent deaths. We read of conspiracies on the part of patricians and others. A few illustrations will show the spirit of the age. King Eadbert became a monk.[4] He gave up the kingdom to his son

[1] S.D. p. 13. Cf. *ibid.* p. 141, for an anonymous writer's statement that Ceolwulf gave up his kingdom and his wife, and then " betook himself with a great treasure to the monastery of Lindisfarne, laid aside his beard, and received the tonsure."

[2] *V. inf.* pp. 25-26.

[3] H. & S. iii. 447-461.

[4] *Baedae Continuatio, s.a.* 758.

4 RELIGIOUS LIFE IN THE 8TH CENTURY

Osulf. In language which is a model of terseness, we
are told that the new king both held and lost the
kingdom in one year, as he was " wickedly slain by
his own household." [1] Ethelwald (Moll) was the
next king. In the course of his reign, he was opposed
by a *dux* named Oswine. A battle was fought at
Eildon, near Melrose, and Oswine was slain. [2] Kings
themselves did not hesitate to compass the deaths of
possible rivals to the throne. Alcuin's letters corroborate, and sometimes expand, what we learn from
Symeon of Durham. *E.g.* Ethelred became king in
A.D. 774, but after a few years was dethroned and
driven into exile. During his brief reign, he had
contrived the death of three *duces*. Restored to the
throne in A.D. 790, he once more resorted to bloodshed.
He ordered the death of a former king named Osred.
He ordered that Eardulf (who subsequently became
king) should be slain outside the gate of the monastery
at Ripon. The body of the presumably dead man was
carried by the monks, to the accompaniment of
Gregorian chants, and placed in a tent outside the
church, but after midnight he was found alive inside
the sacred building. [3] Another instance of cruelty on
Ethelred's part is recorded with regard to the sons of
Elfwald (a former king who was slain as the result of a
conspiracy made by a patrician named Sicgan).
They were treacherously slain. [4]

[1] S.D. pp. 20-21.   [2] *Ibid.* p. 21. Cf. *A.S.C. s.a.* 761.
[3] S.D. p. 30. Alcuin, in a letter which he wrote to Eardulf, alludes
to this deliverance from death. Mon. Alc. p. 304.   [4] S.D. l.c.

We have not yet come to an end of the tale of blood-shed. In A.D. 796, Ethelred himself was slain at a place called Cobre (probably Corbridge, near Hexham).[1] We can hardly feel surprised when Alcuin says that he had not found the mind of the king such as he had hoped or wished.[2] He wrote two letters, full of earnest exhortations, to him and to his nobles.[3] In a letter which he wrote to Offa, king of Mercia (Ethelred's father-in-law [4]), he tells of the indignation felt by Charles, king of the Franks, on hearing the news of the murder. Charles was on the point of despatching gifts to Ethelred and to the Northumbrian sees. He withdrew the intended gifts, and in his anger he denounced the Northumbrians as " that treacherous and perverse people, slayer of their own lords." [5] The above tragedy in Northumbria also affected Alcuin's own plans. He had intended to return to his native land, but now he decided other-wise. " It seemed better to me, for the sake of the peace of my nation, to continue on pilgrimage ; not knowing what I could have done among people in whose midst no one is secure, or able to prevail in any wholesome counsel. Lo ! the most holy places have been laid waste by pagans, the altars defiled by perjuries, the monasteries violated by adulteries, the land polluted with the blood of lords and princes." [6]

[1] S.D., pp. 33–34, and note.
[2] Mon. Alc. p. 172.
[3] Ibid. pp. 180–190.
[4] S.D. p. 31, and note.
[5] Mon. Alc. p. 290.
[6] Ibid. p. 291.

After Ethelred's death, a patrician named Osbald held the kingship for twenty-seven days. But he was deserted by his chief supporters, and took refuge, first in the island of Lindisfarne, and afterwards with the king of the Picts.[1] Alcuin wrote a letter, beseeching him to go into a monastery, and not to "add sin upon sin in laying waste his country and in shedding of blood."[2] The counsel seems to have prevailed, because Osbald ended his days as an abbot, and was buried in the church at York.[3]

Osbald's brief tenure of power being over, Eardulf ascended the throne. Alcuin writes to him in the usual tone of exhortation.[4] The letter is not devoid of hope that he will inaugurate a new era in Northumbria. The king is addressed as one who, in the writer's judgment, had been preserved for better times. But another letter (not addressed to Eardulf) is less hopeful. He there expresses a fear lest that king will soon lose his kingdom, owing to the offence which he gives to God by his conduct in putting away his own wife and publicly (so it was said) associating himself with a concubine.[5]

Towards the end of the century, the raids of the Northmen began. Alcuin dwells on the shame and the horror of these raids. "A very great danger," he writes, " is hanging over this island and the people who dwell in it. Lo ! a thing which was never heard

---

[1] S.D. p. 34.   [2] Mon. Alc. pp. 305-306.   [3] S. D. p. 37.
[4] Mon. Alc. pp. 303-305.   [5] Ibid. p. 350.

of before, a pagan people is in the habit of laying waste our shores with piracy and robbery." [1] Similarly, " the pagans in times past did not attempt to sail over our sea and to devastate the shores of our country. It is a kind of punishment or warning, that we may fear God and in a better way keep His commandments." [2] The dark cloud was rendered even darker by the internal dissensions which prevailed. " The English peoples and realms and kings are at disagreement among themselves. Scarcely any one now—I cannot say it without tears—is found who belongs to the ancient lineage of kings. The more uncertain their origin, the less their bravery." [3] Almost everywhere, he tells us, the royal race has gone, unknown persons being exalted, and the more prudent counsellors being taken away.[4] There was national danger and degeneracy. " From the days of King Elfwald, fornications, adulteries, and incests have swept in a flood over the land . . . what shall I say of avarice, rapines, and violent judgments ? " [5] In a similar strain is a letter which he wrote to Offa.[6] As he viewed the state of society in his native land, he could indeed call it a time of " tribulation." [7] He states that the Northumbrian kingdom " has almost perished because of internal dissensions and false swearings," nor does it seem to him " that there is yet an end

---

[1] Mon. Alc. p. 371.

[3] *Ibid.* p. 371.

[5] *Ibid.* pp. 181-182. [6] *V. sup.* p. 5.

[2] *Ibid.* p. 373.

[4] *Ibid.* p. 373.

[7] Mon. Alc. pp. 349, 353.

to the evil doing of those men." [1] He quote. Gildas's statement of the sins which caused the Britons to lose their land, and he considers that the story should be taken as a warning. [2]

There was one particular incident in connection with the Northmen's raids which made a deep impression on the mind of Alcuin, and which he repeatedly uses as a solemn warning to amendment of life, viz. the destruction of Lindisfarne (A.D. 793). The Anglo-Saxon Chronicler, in language the brevity of which in no wise detracts from its impressiveness, says : " the havoc of heathen men miserably destroyed God's church at Lindisfarne, through rapine and slaughter." [3] A graphic account of the tragedy is given by Symeon of Durham. [4] After telling of the sacrilege and pillage, he tells the fate which overtook the monks, some being slain, some being bound and led away captive, some being cast forth naked, some being drowned. Alcuin also gives details, and enlarges on the lessons to be learnt. [5] " The church of S. Cuthbert was sprinkled with the blood of the priests of God, and spoiled of all its ornaments. . . . Foxes have plundered the chosen vine, the heritage of the Lord has been given to a people not His own . . . *ubi laus Domini, ibi ludus gentium.*" [6] In a similar strain, " pagans have polluted the sanctuaries of God and poured out the blood of

[1] Mon. Alc. p. 351. [2] *Ibid.* pp. 206, 371.
[3] *A.S.C. s.a.* 793. [4] S.D. p. 32.
[5] Mon. Alc. pp. 181, 183, 189–194, 198–199.
[6] *Ibid.* p. 181.

saints around the altar, have laid waste the house of our hope, have trodden the bodies of saints in the temple of God as it were a dunghill in the street." [1] He points the moral. "Fear the scourge," he says, "which has come upon the church of S. Cuthbert— a most holy place, and long kept most safe by the prayers of many saints, but now miserably devastated by pagans. He who does not fear this, and does not correct himself, and does not cry to God for the prosperity of his country, has a heart not of flesh but of stone." [2] *Morum emendatio*, he says, was of greater power than *armorum congregatio*.[3] He himself promises to use his influence with King Charles on behalf of the boys led away captive by the pagans.[4]

A raid attempted by the Northmen in the following year was by no means so successful. They had entered the estuary known as the Port of Egfrid, and had plundered Jarrow. Retribution, however, soon overtook them. Their leader was slain. A storm arose which "shook, destroyed, and crushed" their ships. Many of the raiders were drowned. Some of them were cast ashore and ruthlessly slain. The Chronicler's comment is: "these things rightly happened to them, since they grievously injured persons who were not injuring them." [5]

[1] Mon. Alc. p. 190.   [2] *Ibid.* p. 189.
[3] *Ibid.* p. 194.   Cf. *ibid.* pp. 198–199.   [4] *Ibid.* pp. 192–193.
[5] S.D. pp. 32–33.

MERCIA

The letters of Boniface and of Alcuin give us much information about various Mercian kings.

1. *Ceolred* (A.D. 709–716). William of Malmesbury speaks of this king as being " wonderful in valour against Ini, but pitiable in his immature death." [1] In a vision seen by a monk of Wenlock, and narrated by Boniface to Eadburga (abbess of S. Mildred, Thanet), there is a dreadful tale—Ceolred was still alive at the time—about the fate of that king's soul. [2] Angels and demons were contending for its possession, and the demons won the day. No useful purpose would be served by giving further details. [3]

In the admonitory letter addressed to Ethelbald, king of Mercia, Ceolred is charged—in common with Osred, king of Northumbria—with violating the privileges of churches. [4] The writers go on to speak, by way of warning to Ethelbald, of the terrible fate which overtook these two kings. Of Osred we have spoken before. [5] Of Ceolred it was reported by eye-witnesses that he was holding a splendid feast with his nobles, when an evil spirit suddenly drove him mad, so that " without penitence and confession, raging and

---

[1] G.R. i. 79. Cf. Eddius, c. 64 (Wilfrid's intended visit to Ceolred).

[2] Mon. Mog. pp. 59–60.

[3] Cf. the vision in which Wilfrid saw King Egfrid's soul carried off by two evil spirits. Eadmer, *Vita Wilf.* cc. 43, 57.

[4] Mon. Mog. p. 174.

[5] *V. sup.* pp. 1–2.

out of his mind, holding converse with devils and
spurning the priests of God, he departed from the light
of this life, doubtless to the torments of hell." [1]

2. *Ethelbald* (A.D. 716–757). This king occupied a
position of paramount importance in the island.[2] He
is represented by the Continuator of Bede (*s.a.* 740)
as laying waste part of Northumbria "by wicked
fraud," whilst King Eadbert was away fighting against
the Picts. In the *Anglo-Saxon Chronicle*, we read about
his wars.[3] His miserable death is also recorded.[4]

Some contradictory elements appear in his character.
In the admonitory letter referred to above, the writers
speak approvingly of several things which they had
heard about him—his almsgiving, his prohibition of
theft, etc., his defence of widows and of the poor, the
peace which was established in his kingdom.[5] But
sorrowful mention is made of the report that he had
violated privileges of churches and of monasteries.[6]
It seems strange that Ethelbald should have been
guilty of such acts of violation. If the statements of
the Evesham chronicler can be trusted, the king would
seem to have been, early in his reign, a generous
benefactor to the recently founded monastery.[7] One
of his grants was in a place "where salt waters bubble

[1] Mon. Mog. p. 175.
[2] H.E. v. 23 (with Plummer's note *a.l.*).
[3] A.S.C. *s.a.* 741, 743, 752.
[4] *Ibid. s.a.* 757. Cf. S.D. p. 20.
[5] Mon. Mog. p. 169.
[6] *Ibid.* p. 174.
[7] *Chron. Evesham*, pp. 72–73. R.S.

up," and so was a source of considerable revenue. We cannot, however, press the statements of the chronicler unduly, because the two Evesham charters in which these grants occur have been considered to be spurious.[1] There are several other ecclesiastical charters, not relating to Evesham, which were issued by Ethelbald.[2] He presided at a Council which guaranteed the complete " liberty, honour, authority, and security of the Church of Christ."[3] To much the same effect, he published what might well be called a charter of ecclesiastical and monastic liberty.[4]

One other report caused much grief to the writers, viz. that Ethelbald never had a lawfully wedded wife, but was guilty of flagrant immoralities (mainly with nuns). The nature of the sin of fornication is pointed out. " It is more serious and worse than almost all sins, and truly can be called the noose of death, the pit of hell, and the abyss of destruction."[5] In a remarkably eloquent passage, the writers dwell upon the national degeneracy which is the inevitable result of immorality. The whole people would become more and more decadent, until at last they would " neither be brave in war nor steadfast in faith, neither honourable in the sight of men nor lovable in the sight of God."[6]

---

[1] *K.C.D.* lxv., lxviii. The fatal asterisk (denoting that the document is a forgery or liable to suspicion) is prefixed to both charters.

[2] *Ibid.* lxxv., lxxix., lxxx., lxxxiii., xc., ci.

[3] H. & S. iii. 341.

[4] *Ibid.* iii. 386-387.

[5] Mon. Mog. pp. 169-171.

[6] *Ibid.* p. 173.

3. *Offa* (A.D. 757–796). " He won the Mercian kingdom with a blood-stained sword." In these words, the Continuator of Bede would seem to be alluding to the civil war and to Offa's victory over Beornred.[1]

In Alcuin's letters we find many references to Offa. Of special interest is what we read about his relations with Charles, king of the Franks. At one time there had been dissension between them. This quarrel was inflamed, says Alcuin, by diabolical influence, and it had the unfortunate result of stopping maritime trade on both sides.[2] The quarrel put Alcuin himself in a difficult position. He had never been unfaithful, he explains, to Offa and the English people, but would serve, to the best of his power, both his friends abroad and those whom he had left at home.[3] The quarrel, happily, was composed. We have a letter written by Charles to Offa, which is marked throughout by a spirit of friendship and of respect.[4] Two interesting points in the letter relate to (*a*) pilgrims on their way to Rome, (*b*) English and Frankish merchants.

(*a*) Charles professes his willingness to grant, as he had done in the past, all facilities to *bonâ fide* pilgrims. But he had discovered that in the ranks of these pilgrims there were people who made the journey for

---

[1] Cf. S.D. p. 20. For Offa's grants to the Church, see *K.C.D.* cxix., cxx., cxxii., cxxiii., cxxxiv.

[2] Mon. Alc. p. 167.

[3] *Ibid.* p. 169.

[4] *Ibid.* pp. 286–289.

the sake of opportunities of unlicensed merchandise, " seekers after gain, not servants of religion." Such persons were to pay the usual tolls, but the others were to be freed from such tolls.

(*b*) English merchants, pursuing lawful trade in the Frankish kingdom, were to enjoy the royal protection. Any cases of oppression were to be referred to himself or the judges (just as an appeal should be made to Offa, if there was oppression of Frankish merchants in that king's jurisdiction).

Indeed, the relationship between these two powerful monarchs would seem to have been most cordial. Alcuin, writing to Offa, says : " King Charles has often spoken lovingly and faithfully with me about you, and in him you have in all respects a most faithful friend." [1]

Personally, Alcuin appears to have entertained a very high opinion of Offa. This was doubtless due, in large measure, to the fact that the king was a supporter of learning. Alcuin once sent him a pupil of his own, with careful instructions as to how that pupil was to be treated.[2] He pronounces a eulogy on the king, who had such a zeal for learning " that the lamp of wisdom shone in his kingdom, although now extinguished in many places." He was " the glory of Britain," and an exhortation is given " to have God always before his eyes, to do justice, and to love mercy." In another letter, he is addressed as " the most wise governor of the people of God," and an even

---

[1] Mon. Alc. p. 290.   [2] *Ibid.* p. 265.

longer exhortation is given.[1] In yet another letter, we read of some person (seemingly an abbot) who was the victim of persecution. Alcuin states that he had written invoking the protection of Offa on his behalf.[2]

There are one or two passages, however, which show that Alcuin had not an altogether unqualified admiration for Offa's doings.[3] Writing, after the king's death, to Osbert the patrician (who had been the royal minister),[4] he alludes approvingly to the late king's legislation.[5] But he also alludes to bloodshed caused by him.[6] Writing to Cenwulf, king of Mercia, he exhorts him to follow up Offa's good deeds. But the new king was to avoid anything that the former king might have done in a spirit of avarice or of cruelty.[7]

The widespread nature of Offa's influence may be illustrated by two incidents :

(a) Charles writes to him with regard to a Scottish priest who was then in the diocese of Cologne, and who was accused of having eaten flesh in Lent. It is requested that this priest should be removed and sent to be tried by the ecclesiastical authorities in his own country.[8]

[1] Mon. Alc. pp. 291-292.
[2] *Ibid.* p. 266.
[3] William of Malmesbury (G.R. i. 84) says that his mind is in doubt, when considering Offa's deeds, whether to approve or to disapprove. That king's character seemed to him to be paradoxical.
[4] For a grant of land made by Offa to Osbert, see *K.C.D.* cliii.
[5] Mon. Alc. p. 351.
[6] *Ibid.* p. 350.
[7] *Ibid.* pp. 352-353.
[8] H. & S. iii. 486-487.

(*b*) Some English exiles had taken refuge with Charles.[1] He asks the persons to whom he addresses a letter that they would intercede with Offa on behalf of these exiles. He somewhat naïvely remarks that, if the intercession fails, " it is better to remain on pilgrimage than to perish, to serve in a strange country than to die in one's own." [2]

4. *Cenwulf* (A.D. 796–819). Offa was succeeded by his son, Egferth.[3] This young man died after a reign of one hundred and forty-one days. His untimely death is evidently regarded by Alcuin as a punishment for the blood which his father had shed.[4] Cenwulf then came to the throne. He was a vigorous and powerful ruler.[5] Exhortations of the usual sort are addressed to him by Alcuin.[6] We can see that the writer's mind was uneasy, as he viewed the condition of his country. " The English people," he says, " because of their sins are burdened with many tribulations." [7]

Cenwulf's relationship with the Papacy, as shown by the letters which passed between him and Pope Leo III., will be considered at a later stage.[8]

[1] H. & S. iii. 488, *n. a.*
[2] *Ibid.* iii. 487–488.
[3] Egferth's character and conduct are warmly commended by William of Malmesbury (G.R. i. 93–94).
[4] Mon. Alc. pp. 3.10, 253.
[5] S.D. pp. 34–55 ; G.R. i. 95. Extravagant praise is lavished upon him (G.R. i. 94–95).
[6] Mon, Alc. pp. 352–354.
[7] *Ibid.* p. 355.
[8] *V. inf.* pp. 30–31.

KENT

In comparison with Northumbria and Mercia, we learn little from our letters about affairs in Kent. We have a letter from Ethelbert II., king of Kent (A.D. 748–760), to Boniface.[1] It reveals the king's fondness for falconry, and it is interesting in some other respects, but it throws no light on the political situation.

The chronology of the Kentish kings in the later part of the century is obscure.[2] We hear a good deal about the troubles during the reign of Eadbert Praen (A.D. 796–798).[3] It was in consequence of these troubles that Ethelheard, archbishop of Canterbury, fled from his see.[4] Alcuin writes to the Kentish people in the hope that they will recall their archbishop. " It is not good," he says, " that the see of S. Augustine our first preacher should remain vacant." [5] In what may almost seem to be exaggerated language, he dwells on the old-time glory of the Kentish kingdom, and he contrasts the present with the past.[6] To Ethelheard himself he writes a cautiously worded letter, but it is clear that he did not approve of the archbishop's

---

[1] Mon. Mog. pp. 254–256.
[2] G.R. i. 18, *n*. 1.
[3] H. & S. iii. 496, *n*. a.
[4] Ethelheard succeeded Jaenbert. Formerly he had been abbot "Hludensis monasterii" (S.D. p. 30). On identification of this monastery, cf. H. & S. iii. 468, *n*. a.
[5] Mon. Alc. p. 372.
[6] *Ibid.* pp. 370–371.

C

conduct in seeking flight. He recommends that penance should be done.[1]

The unfortunate Eadbert Praen fell under the condemnation of Pope Leo III., who branded him as an apostate, and likened him to Julian.[2] Eventually, he was captured by Cenwulf, king of Mercia, who had invaded Kent with a powerful army, and had ravaged that kingdom. He wreaked a savage vengeance upon Eadbert, ordering his eyes to be put out and his hands to be cut off. So, at least, says Symeon of Durham.[3] We do not read, however, of any of these barbarities in William of Malmesbury's narrative. Eadbert, we are there told, was led away captive, but was liberated on the day of the dedication of the abbey church at Winchcombe.[4]

[1] Mon. Alc. pp. 366-369.
[2] *Ibid.* p. 365.
[3] S.D. p. 35.
[4] G.R. i. 94-95. Cf. *ibid.* i. 18.

CHAPTER II

RELATIONS WITH ROME

(i) MISSIONARY WORK OF BONIFACE

THE Papacy comes into great prominence in connection with English missionary efforts on the Continent of Europe. It may be objected that this subject does not fall within the scope of English religious life in the eighth century. But a little reflection will show that the two subjects are closely interwoven. It was an Englishman, Willibrord, who continued the missionary work which had been begun in the previous century by Wilfrid. It was an Englishman, Winfrid (better known as Boniface) who went as a missionary to Frisia and to pagan peoples in Germany. After he had suffered martyrdom (A.D. 754), the work was continued by another Englishman, Lullus. Nothing, perhaps, strikes us more, in reading the correspondence carried on by Boniface and Lullus with friends at home, than the frequency with which the writers ask for the prayers of their English friends. It was from England that the ranks of the missionaries were recruited. The writers were upheld in their difficult task by the knowledge that they had the interest and the sympathy of friends at home. In fact, England may be regarded as the "home base" for this Continental work. There was a close link between English religious life and the work of these voluntary "exiles for Christ."

It is here that the part played by the Papacy comes in. Had it not been for the support afforded by the Papacy, much of the missionary work, humanly speaking, would have been impossible. Boniface went to Rome, was favourably received by Pope Gregory II., and obtained that pontiff's sanction for his enterprise.[1] It is interesting to note the *authority* on which this sanction was based and the *terms* in which it was given. The Pope, after some complimentary language about Boniface's conduct in seeking the counsel of the Apostolic See, and after an exposition of the relationship subsisting between the head and the members, gives his sanction "in the Name of the Indivisible Trinity, by the unbroken authority of the blessed Peter, chief of the Apostles."[2] He goes on to authorise Boniface to preach to "peoples held in the error of infidelity, to whom he may be able by God's help to come." He was "by the spirit of virtue and of love and of sobriety, to instil in a suitable manner the preaching of both Testaments into untaught minds."

For a few years, Boniface co-operated with Willibrord in Frisia. Then he entered upon the work with

---

[1] Cf. H.E. v. 11, for sanction given to Willibrord by Pope Sergius I.
[2] Mon. Mog. p. 63.

which his memory is imperishably associated, viz. among pagan peoples in Germany. He was consecrated a bishop on S. Andrew's Day, 722, at Rome.[1] The Papacy again proved a most valuable support. Gregory II. wrote various commendatory letters.[2] One of them was to the famous Charles Martel, and requested the aid of the temporal authority for the missionary in his work. Another letter is addressed to " all Christians who fear God." Blessings and anathemas are pronounced. The former were for persons who helped Boniface, the latter were for persons who opposed him. We have a letter in which Papal replies are given to questions submitted by Boniface.[3] Gregory II. approves of this consultation as to " the belief and teaching of this Holy Apostolic Roman Church." He states that " the blessed Apostle Peter was the beginning of the Apostolate and the Episcopate," while he himself (i.e. the Pope) does not speak by his own authority, but " by the grace of Him Who opens the mouth of the dumb and makes the tongues of infants to speak."

It is impossible to read the correspondence of Boniface without seeing that the relationship between him and the Papacy was of the closest kind. He had taken a most solemn oath, in which he bound himself

---

[1] *Vita Bonf.* c. 6. Some ten years later, he was made an archbishop, and received the pall, with directions as to the occasions on which he was to use it (Mon. Mog. p. 92).

[2] Mon. Mog. pp. 77 ff.

[3] *Ibid.* pp. 88-91.

to keep the Catholic Faith, to take no steps against the unity of the Church, to bear allegiance to S. Peter, his Vicar Pope Gregory II. and his successors.[1] From time to time, he wrote to successive Popes— Gregory II., Gregory III., Zacharias—reporting the progress of the mission, and seeking guidance in difficulties. He describes himself as " the German legate of the Universal Church, and the servant of the Apostolic See," and as " the German legate of the Catholic, Apostolic, Roman Church." [2]   Gregory III. describes him as filling the position of Papal *vicarius* (*Bonifatium, nostram agentem vicem*).[3]   Similarly, Zacharias speaks of him as having been appointed to preach in those parts *vice nostra*.[4]   Of his allegiance to the Papacy there can be no doubt.   Not very long before his martyrdom, he wrote to Pope Stephen III., and professed his wish " to remain his faithful and devoted servant in the same manner in which he had previously served the Apostolic See under the two Gregorys and Zacharias, who always strengthened and helped him by their exhortation and by the authority of their letters."   Any service which he had rendered to the Papacy during the past thirty-six years, he wished to continue and increase, any deficiencies he wished promptly and humbly to amend.[5]

[1] Mon. Mog. pp. 76–77.
[2] *Ibid.* pp. 107, 200.
[3] *Ibid.* p. 103.
[4] *Ibid.* p. 153.   Cf. *ibid.* p. 194, " nostram praesentantem vicem."
[5] *Ibid.* p. 259.

It does not fall within our province to trace in detail
the story of Boniface's labours. Suffice it to say that
the enterprise caused a wider outlook on the part of
the English Church. Volunteers came out from home,
mainly, it would seem, from the West-Saxon country,
where Boniface's fame as a scholar and a teacher would
still survive. One of these recruits was Lullus,[1] whose
personal piety and interest in learning are abundantly
shown in the correspondence carried on with friends
at home. He proved to be a most loyal disciple and
colleague. We read of a presbyter of Glastonbury
who went out and came to the borders of Hesse and
Saxony. He wrote a letter to the members of the
monastery, telling how Boniface had come a long way
to meet him, and of the welcome received at his
hands.[2] Cuthbert, archbishop of Canterbury, testifies
to the attainments of the helpers. It is a source of
legitimate pride that England sent out " many well-
educated and excellently instructed disciples." [3] Some
of them, we are told by Willibald,[4] were readers,
others were writers, others were educated in various
arts. He adds that they were scattered widely in
Hesse and in Thuringia, preaching the Word of
God.

We shall notice later some of the requests for prayer
which Boniface made to friends at home, particularly
his special request for the prayers of *all* English

[1] Mon. Mog. pp. 109-110. [2] *Ibid.* p. 246.
[3] *Ibid.* p. 263. [4] *Vita Bonf.* l.c.

Christians.[1] Nor can we doubt that many prayers on his behalf were offered in English churches and monasteries. An East-Anglian king named Elfwald assures him that his name will be remembered at the Services of the Canonical Hours in the monasteries of the East-Anglian kingdom.[2] Cuthbert writes a beautiful consolatory letter to Lullus on the occasion of Boniface's death.[3] The letter shows the interest taken in the missionary work, and the writer announces the decision of the English Church that the anniversary of Boniface's death should henceforth be a day of solemn celebration.

In thinking of the beneficent results of the above mission, including the ways in which it affected English religious life, we cannot withhold a recognition of the part played by the Papacy. It was Papal support, as we have seen, which did much to make Boniface's task possible. The Popes were always interested in the progress of his work, and ready to be his counsellors. In view of all the circumstances of the case, we can understand the almost exaggerated spirit of deference which he showed to the Papacy. How far the Popes may have been influenced by other motives besides missionary zeal, it is impossible to say. The fact remains that Gregory II., Gregory III., and Zacharias did much to render possible the evangelisation of large parts of Germany.

[1] *V. inf.* p. 77.   [2] Mon. Mog. p. 211.
[3] *Ibid.* pp. 261–266 ; H. & S. iii. 390–394.

(ii) PAPAL LEGATION TO ENGLAND

The very name of Papal legates has an evil connotation in England. It calls to mind the pecuniary exactions which were practised in the reign of Henry III. But the legation with which we are now concerned was free from many of the objectionable features which characterised its successors in the Middle Ages. A brief allusion has been made to it in the previous chapter.[1] We may now give fuller details.

Symeon of Durham, under the year 786, has the following notice :—" At that time legates were sent by the Apostolic See from the Lord Pope Adrian to Britain, among whom the venerable bishop George held the first place ; who renewed ancient friendship among us, and the Catholic Faith which S. Gregory the Pope taught by the blessed Augustine ; who were honourably received by the kings, governors, and leading men of this country, and in peace returned home with great gifts, as was just." [2] The legates were George, bishop of Ostia, and Theophylact, bishop of Todi. In a letter which they wrote to the Pope, they describe their experiences.[3] They landed safely in England after a stormy voyage, and were received by Jaenbert, archbishop of Canterbury. Then they proceeded to the court of Offa, king of Mercia. He honourably received the legates and the

[1] *V. sup.* p. 3. [2] S.D. p. 29. Cf. *A.S.C. s.a.* 785.
[3] H. & S. iii. 447-461.

letters which they had brought from the Apostolic
See "with great joy, because of his veneration for the
blessed Peter and the Papal Apostolate." Everything
seemed to go smoothly. Cynewulf, king of the West-
Saxons, met with Offa in council.[1] After a time,
George went off to Northumbria. A synod was held
in that kingdom. We are fortunate in having a
detailed list of the canons which were unanimously
accepted at that synod, and to which we have the
attestations of the leading persons present. The same
canons were afterwards unanimously accepted at a
Southern synod, and again we have a list of attestations.

The above canons—as set forth in the legates' letter
—constitute a most important document. We do not
summarise them here, as they deserve to be read in
full. There can be no doubt that such canons, if
faithfully observed, would have tended to a reformation
of English life and morals. We are especially struck
by the high standard of ministerial responsibility which
is inculcated. Canon III. (on the duty of bishops)
will well repay perusal. Among other striking passages in the document is Canon XX. (on conversion,
penitence, and confession). In several cases, an
interesting sidelight is thrown upon English religious
and social life :

(a) The bishops are exhorted to check such practices

---

[1] On Cynewulf's tragic death, see S.D. p. 28. We have a letter
(Mon. Mog. pp. 306-307) written by him and his leading men to
Lullus.

as augury, sooth-saying, incantations, divinations, etc.[1]
The writers refer to the report that in time of litigation
it was the custom, " after the manner of the Gentiles,"
to cast lots, and they condemn such a practice as being
sacrilege.[2]

It may not be amiss at this point to say something
about the vitality of paganism. Both in our own land
and on the Continent, the process of Christianisation
was slow and difficult. There was a wonderful
vitality about pagan rites ; and, even where they had
been suppressed, there was always a danger of their
recrudescence. The Christianity of many people,
doubtless, was little more than nominal, or of the most
superficial kind. It was only through the help of the
Frankish temporal power, Boniface tells us, that he was
able to prohibit pagan rites and the sacrilegious
worship of idols in Germany. It was " fear "—he
himself uses the word—rather than conviction that was
operative.[3]

Willibald gives an account of Boniface's early
labours among the Hessians.[4] Some of these people
secretly, others openly, adhered to pagan rites, sacri-
ficing in groves and at fountains, practising augury,
divination, and such-like ; whilst others, " casting

---

[1] H. & S. iii. 449. Cf. ibid. iii. 410, where it is laid down (Dialogue
of Egbert) that persons guilty of such practices as some of the above were
not to be ordained, or, if ordained, they were to be deposed.
[2] Ibid. iii. 458–459.
[3] Mon. Mog. p. 159.
[4] Vita Bonf. l.c.

away every profanation of the Gentiles, did none of these things." The same biographer tells us about the cutting down of a sacred tree, in the presence of a great company of pagans, at Geismar.[1]

Pope Gregory III., in a letter which he wrote to the German peoples, gives a list of practices which were " to be altogether cast away and rejected." [2] In the Capitulary of Carloman, we find even fuller particulars.[3] Boniface writes to Cuthbert, archbishop of Canterbury, giving an account of a Council which he had held. It was there decided that each bishop once a year should go carefully over his diocese. He was " to investigate and prohibit pagan observances, divination, casting of lots, auguries, amulets, incantations, and all uncleannesses of the Gentiles." [4]

We read of backsliding Christians in our own land during a pestilence of the previous century. They resorted to such pagan rites as incantations and the wearing of amulets.[5] The Council of Clovesho dealt with the subject of pagan observances in language almost identical with that of the passage which we are now considering.[6]

[1] *Vita Bonf.* l.c. On the Teutonic religion, see a suggestive article entitled " The condition of the German Provinces as illustrating the methods of St. Boniface," in *J.T.S.*, Oct. 1905.
[2] Mon. Mog. p. 102.
[3] H. & S. iii. 385.
[4] Mon. Mog. p. 202.
[5] H.E. iv. 27.
[6] H. & S. iii. 363-364. [In all cases where mention is made in this work of the Council of Clovesho, the reference is to the famous Council which met in A.D. 747.]

(b) Various regulations were made with a view to seemliness at the celebration of Mass. One of these regulations was to the effect that the paten and chalice should not be made of the horn of an ox.[1]

(c) False weights and measures are prohibited, and payment of tithes is enjoined. All persons were to give the tenth of all they possessed, because it " specially belonged to the Lord God." They were to live on the remaining nine-tenths, out of which they were to give alms. On the non-payment of tithes, we have the pithy remark—*plerumque contingit, ut qui decimam non tribuit, ad decimam revertitur.*[2]

(d) Disfigurement of horses—e.g. amputation of tails—is condemned, so is the widespread practice of eating horseflesh.[3]

(iii) King Cenwulf (Mercia) and Pope Leo III.

The see of Lichfield at one time included the whole of Mercia and of the Mid-Anglian kingdom. On the death (A.D. 737) of Aldwine, bishop of Lichfield, Hwitta was made bishop of Lichfield, and Totta

---

[1] The passage (H. & S. iii. 452) would seem to mean that horn was objected to because it was " sanguineum."

[2] *Ibid.* iii. 456–457.

[3] *Ibid.* iii. 458–459. For Papal prohibition of eating the flesh of horses (either wild or domestic), a practice which prevailed in some parts of the Continent, see Mon. Mog. p. 93. The practice is called unclean and detestable."

bishop of Leicester.[1] Through the influence of Offa, the former see was elevated to metropolitan dignity, Higbert receiving the pall from Pope Adrian I.[2] The creation of this metropolitanate involved a great diminution of the privileges and the prestige of Jaenbert, archbishop of Canterbury. Alcuin deplores the step. It seemed to him a breach in the unity of the Church, and he was very dubious as to the validity of the reasons which had brought about the creation of an archbishopric at Lichfield. In order to heal the breach by peaceable means, he was in favour of holding a joint deliberation of all the clergy—the archbishop of York being associated with the archbishop of Canterbury—but he was not in favour of Higbert being deprived of the pall in his lifetime, although he wished the consecration of bishops once more to revert to Canterbury.[3]

Cenwulf wrote a letter to Pope Leo III.[4] After a long and wearisome exordium, we come to the main point of the letter, which is the derogation from the rights of Canterbury. To the writer it seemed that the association of Canterbury with the burial-place of Augustine pointed to that city as the fitting place for the metropolitanate. Although professing to blame

---

[1] S.D. p. 13. In Mon. Mog. p. 252 *n*., it is pointed out that Totta is the same person as Torthelm, bishop of Leicester, who writes a letter to Boniface.

[2] On these proceedings, cf. G.R. i. 85, G.P. pp. 15–16.

[3] Mon. Alc. pp. 368–369.

[4] H. & S. iii. 521–523.

neither Offa nor Adrian, he really does so in effect.
Offa, he says, was actuated by his quarrel with Jaenbert
and the Kentish people, whilst Adrian " at the request
of the aforesaid king, began to do what no one previously presumed to do, and exalted the Mercian
bishop with the pall." [1] To this letter Pope Leo III.
sent a reply. [2] It is of a somewhat unconvincing
character in its defence of the action of his predecessor,
Adrian I. Indeed, it would seem that the Pope was
not altogether pleased with Cenwulf regarding another
matter referred to in the letter. Offa had once vowed
(as a thank-offering for victory) to send a yearly sum
to the Roman See—one *mancus* for every day of the
year—and this vow was to be binding on his successors. The contribution, however, which Cenwulf
had recently despatched only amounted to about
one-third of that sum.

The final stages of the dispute between Canterbury
and Lichfield do not fall within the scope of our
inquiry. The Mercian archbishopric was abolished in
A.D. 802. No person since Higbert has borne the title
of archbishop of Lichfield. [3]

[1] William of Malmesbury (G.P. p. 16) hints at the possibility of gifts
from Offa to Pope Adrian I.
[2] H. & S. iii. 523-525 ; Mon. Alc. pp. 363-366.
[3] William of Malmesbury (G.P. p. 307) speaks disparagingly of
Lichfield as a site for a bishopric,

(iv) Pilgrimages to Rome

Several instances are recorded of English pilgrimages to Rome in the seventh century. The classical instance, of course, is that of Benedict Biscop. He paid no fewer than *six* visits, although, on the third occasion, he did not go direct from England.[1] On his fifth visit, he was accompanied by Ceolfrid.[2] Another early pilgrim was Wilfrid.[3] He and Benedict Biscop travelled together as far as to Lyons, where a separation took place. We are fortunate in possessing a fairly full account of Wilfrid's doings in Rome on the occasion of this pilgrimage.[4] *Inter alia*, we read that he paid daily visits to the holy places for the sake of prayer. A royal pilgrim was Caedwalla, who resigned his West-Saxon kingdom, desiring " to be cleansed in the font of baptism at the thresholds of the blessed Apostles." His desire was gratified, and he died soon afterwards.[5]

Instances are also recorded of persons in the seventh century who desired to make the pilgrimage but who could not carry out their intention.[6]

In the eighth century, the stream of English pilgrims became even greater. Bede bears testimony to their numbers—both men and women—and to the various ranks of society from which they were drawn.[7] The

---

[1] H.A.B. § 3. [2] H.A.A. § 10. [3] Eddius, c. 3.
[4] *Ibid.* c. 5. [5] H.E. v. 7.
[6] *Ibid.* iv. 5 (Oswy) ; H.A.B. § 2 (Alchfrid). [7] H.E. v. 7.

West-Saxon king, Ini, went to Rome. He also had resigned his kingdom. " He desired," says Bede, " to dwell as a pilgrim for a time on earth in the neighbourhood of the holy places, so that he might merit a more familiar reception by the saints in heaven." [1] Another royal pilgrim was Cenred of Mercia. Like Caedwalla and Ini, he resigned his kingdom. At Rome, he became a monk, and ended his days in that city. [2] Offa, son of the king of the East-Saxons, also became a monk at Rome. [3]

In some cases the pilgrimage was only intended to be temporary, but in other cases (as we have seen) the pilgrims intended to stay permanently at " the thresholds of the blessed Apostles." [4] The great motive by which the pilgrims were actuated was the desire of personal adoration at the burial-places of the saints, combined with the hope of obtaining the *patrocinium* of these saints.

Contemporary letters will give us several illustrations of eighth-century pilgrimages. Egbert of York had at some time or other been at Rome. [5] We have a letter written by Elfled, abbess of Whitby, in which she commends to a Continental abbess a devoted friend of

---

[1] H.E. l.c. On his conduct in Rome, see G.R. i. 39.

[2] H.E. v. 19.

[3] *Ibid.* l.c.

[4] This had been the intention of King Oswy, if he had been able to go on the Roman pilgrimage. *Ibid.* iv. 5.

[5] *Ep. ad Egb.* § 15. His successor, Albert, also visited Rome (*De Pontif. Ebor.* 1457). So did Daniel, bishop of Winchester (*A.S.C. s.a.* 721), and Forthere, bishop of Sherborne (*ibid. s.a.* 737).

her own who had long desired to visit Rome. This friend "for the love of Christ, and for the honour of the holy apostles, Peter and Paul, was eager to go to their holy thresholds," but hitherto had been detained by Elfled. Now, however, she was able to start on "a journey long desired and often begun." [1] Again, we have another letter, very despondent in tone, written to Boniface by an abbess named Eangyth and her daughter. [2] The loss of friends and kinsfolk is bewailed. Some have died, whilst "others have left their country's shores . . . and sought the thresholds of the holy apostles Peter and Paul, and of many martyrs, virgins, and confessors, whose number and names God knows." The writers themselves wished to go on pilgrimage, and thus express their feelings : "much time has elapsed since we had the desire . . . to seek Rome, once the mistress of the world, and there beg forgiveness of our sins, as many others have done and still do." But they knew that there was opposition in some quarters to the idea of such a pilgrimage. Many people thought that would-be monastic pilgrims should stay at home, each one remaining in the place where vows had been made. The prayers of Boniface were asked, so that God would show the writers whether they should "live in their own land or go into exile on pilgrimage."

The moral danger to which women were exposed on the journey was so great that Boniface thought it

---

[1] Mon. Mog. pp. 49-50.   [2] Ibid. pp. 66-71.

well that women should be altogether forbidden to make such pilgrimages. Writing to Cuthbert, archbishop of Canterbury, he thus speaks of female pilgrims : " To a great extent they perish, few retaining their chastity. There are very few cities in Lombardy, in Francia, and in Gaul, in which there is not an adulteress or a prostitute of English race. This thing is a disgrace and a shame to the whole of your Church." [1]

That Cuthbert's successor, Bregwin, had himself been to Rome is shown by an allusion which he made to his meeting with Lullus in that city. [2] We read of a presbyter named Hunwini who desired to visit Rome, but who died at Beniventum. [3]

We have already noticed the willingness of Charles to grant facilities to pilgrims who passed through the Frankish dominions. [4] Everything, indeed, would seem to indicate that such pilgrimages were a potent factor in the religious life of many of our countrymen and countrywomen in the eighth century. We have a description of Ceolfrid's last journey. [5] It gives us a picture of religious exercises carried on amidst circumstances of great difficulty, and is a striking testimony to the devotion of this pilgrim.

[1] Mon. Mog. p. 208.   [2] *Ibid.* p. 277.
[3] *Ibid.* p. 301.   [4] *V. sup.* p. 13.
[5] H.A.A. §§ 31–33.

CHAPTER III

THE EPISCOPATE

In the *Epistle to Egbert*, Bede paints a somewhat dark picture of Church life in Northumbria. At that time there were four Northumbrian sees—York, Lindisfarne, Hexham, Whithern (Candida Casa).[1] When we consider the vast extent of the Northumbrian kingdom, and the mountainous nature of much of the country, we can recognise the difficulties of the bishops' position. Effective administration and visitation were rendered well-nigh impossible. The parochial system not yet being fully developed, much depended on evangelistic tours undertaken by the bishop himself. Bede alludes to the report that there were many places situated among the mountains and dense woods in which no bishop had been seen for years. Not only was no bishop present who could administer Confirmation in such places, but there was no Christian teacher of any kind.[2] The creation of more sees is advocated. The writer believed that a ready helper would be found in King Ceolwulf, and he advised Egbert to

---

[1] H.E. v. 23. [2] *Ep. ad Egb.* § 7.

consult that true lover of religion.[1] He himself out-
lines a suggestive scheme for the creation of these
sees, and he makes some notable remarks as to their
location.[2] In its essence, this scheme was a revival,
so far as the North was concerned, of Pope Gregory's
scheme of Church organisation, according to which
there was to be a metropolitan at York, with twelve
suffragans.[3]

Bede, it is to be noted, does not write to Egbert in a
spirit of fault-finding, but rather in a spirit of affectionate exhortation. He fully recognises the difficulties of that bishop's task.[4] All the same, he is
evidently trying to rouse him to even greater zeal.

Of *some* bishops, Bede does not speak favourably.
He is speaking of suitable companions as a help
towards the spiritual life. This applied with special
force to bishops. He then alludes to the report that
some bishops kept unsuitable company. Their companions were people who were bound by no restraints
of religion, but were tellers of stories designed to
provoke laughter, were addicted to gluttony and
drunkenness, etc.[5] The passage reminds us of the
advice given by Alcuin to his old pupil, Eanbald II.,
the newly-consecrated archbishop of York. " Let
your companions be men adorned with honourable
principles . . . let them not be followers of drunken-

---

[1] *Ep. ad Egb.* § 9.   [2] *Ibid.* § 10.
[3] *Ibid.* §§ 9–10. Cf. H.E. i. 29.   [4] *Ep. ad Egb.* § 5.
[5] *Ibid.* § 4.

ness, but lovers of sobriety . . . let not vain speaking or scurrility, but holy psalmody, be heard from their mouth. Let them not run about over plains, shouting as they chase foxes ; but, riding with you, let them sweetly chant psalms." [1] Eanbald is also exhorted to be diligent in preaching and in visitation. " Let not your tongue cease in preaching, nor your foot in going round the flock committed to you." [2] This is just the point on which great emphasis is placed by Bede. He implies that the spiritual destitution of people in out-of-the-way parts of Northumbria was largely due to slackness with regard to episcopal visitation. [3] He also brings definite accusations of avarice against some bishops. " Not only do they not preach the Gospel free of charge, or lay hands on the faithful ; but also —which is worse—they receive money from their hearers (which the Lord forbade), and forbear to practise the ministry of the Word (which the Lord commanded)." [4] The neglect of Confirmation—or the inability to administer it—was a circumstance for which the bishops were largely to blame. " Of the whole of this crime there is no cause greater than avarice." [5] When a bishop, owing to the love of money, undertook the charge of a diocese which was too unwieldy to permit of proper episcopal ministrations, he was guilty of great sin. [6] This question of episcopal

[1] Mon. Alc. p. 334.
[2] Ibid. p. 332.
[3] Ep. ad Egb. § 7.
[4] Ibid. l.c.
[5] Ibid. § 8.
[6] Ibid. l.c.

avarice was one with regard to which Eanbald is warned by Alcuin—" be not eager to win gold and silver, but to win souls." [1] In the canons accepted by the legatine synods mentioned in the previous chapter, it is enjoined that no bishop " for the sake of filthy lucre, but for the hope of eternal reward, should seek to feed the flock committed to him." [2]

In the following chapter we shall speak more fully of a subject which caused great grief to Bede, and on which he writes both eloquently and feelingly. This was the existence in Northumbria of many establishments which went, *stilo stultissimo*, by the name of monasteries, but which in no true sense of the term were monasteries. Such places, according to the common saying, were " useful neither to God nor to men." [3] For the foundation and continuance of these so-called monasteries, bishops were not free from blame. [4]

Bede concludes his letter with a solemn warning against avarice. He then adds : " If we wished to treat in like manner of drunkenness, gluttony, wantonness, and the rest of such contagions, the letter would be extended to an immense length." [5] From drunkenness, seemingly, some bishops were not exempt. In Egbert's *Penitential*, there is a warning against this evil on the part of clergy and laity. More specifically, " If any bishop or any ordained person has a customary vice of drunkenness, let him either cease from it or be

---

[1] Mon. Alc. pp. 338-339.   [2] H. & S. iii. 449.
[3] *Ep. ad Egb.* § 11.   [4] *Ibid.* §§ 12-13.   [5] *Ibid.* § 17.

deposed." [1] That such an evil was not merely hypo-
thetical, may be seen from a letter written by Boniface
to Cuthbert, archbishop of Canterbury. He says :
" It is reported also that in your dioceses the evil of
drunkenness is too customary, so that not only do some
bishops not forbid it, but even themselves drinking too
much get intoxicated, and, handing over great cups,
compel others to get intoxicated." After pointing out
the sin of such conduct, he adds : " This evil specially
belongs to pagans and our nation. Neither the Franks
nor the Gauls nor the Lombards nor the Romans nor
the Greeks do this thing." [2]

So far, we have been looking at the darker side of the
picture. Although Bede has hard things to say about
the carelessness, etc., of *some* bishops, it would be a
mistake to assume that he entertained a poor opinion of
the episcopate, as a whole, in the earlier part of the
eighth century. He lovingly portrays the character of
John (bishop of Hexham, and afterwards of York), by
whom he himself had been ordained both to the
diaconate and to the presbyterate. [3] It is true, a large
part of the description is taken up with various works of
healing which are associated with the memory of that
bishop. But it is evident that Bede had a great

---

[1] H. & S. iii. 421, 426.
[2] Mon. Mog. pp. 209-210. This statement is perhaps too sweeping.
Elsewhere, Boniface is speaking about the deplorable state of
ecclesiastical affairs in some parts of the Frankish kingdom. He says
that bishops were found there who were drunkards. *Ibid.* p. 113.
[3] H.E. v. 2-6, 24.

admiration for him. We are told about his piety, his almsgiving, his habit of retiring from time to time for quiet meditation and prayer. Above all, there is infinite tenderness in the picture painted of the good bishop as he sat up all night after the accident to his beloved pupil Heribald, spending the time in prayer.

In Bede's letters to Acca, that bishop is addressed in terms of most affectionate respect.[1] In the *Epistle to Egbert*, we can see the high regard in which Egbert was held by the writer.[2]

Of several bishops outside Northumbria, Bede speaks in high terms. Among his literary helpers who contributed material which he used for his *Ecclesiastical History* were two bishops, Daniel (Winchester) and Cynibert (Lindsey).[3] He mentions the learning of Forthere (Sherborne) and Tobias (Rochester).[4] We do not know if he was personally acquainted with Egwin (Worcester), who would seem to have been a man of wonderful sanctity.[5]

The correspondence of Boniface and of Lullus reveals the episcopate, on the whole, in a favourable light. It would be difficult to exaggerate the value of this correspondence. Many of the letters are of an intimate and personal character, and give us an insight into the spiritual life of the writers. Free mention is

[1] Migne, *P.L.* xciv. 684, 685, 687, 689, 692, 698, 699, 702. Cf. H.E. v. 20.
[2] *Ep. ad Egb.* § 1.   [3] H.E. Pref.
[4] *Ibid.* v. 18, 23.
[5] *Chron. Evesham*, pp. 3 ff. R.S.

made of encouragements and discouragements, and constant requests are made for mutual prayer.

Numerous prelates figure in the above correspondence.

Northern sees.	*York.*	Egbert, Albert=Cena.
	Whithern.	Pecthelm.
Midland sees.	*Leicester.*	Torthelm.
	Worcester.	Milred.
Southern sees.	*Canterbury.*	Nothelm, Cuthbert, Bregwin.
	Winchester.	Daniel, Cyneheard.
	Rochester.	Eardulf.

We do not propose to treat of all the persons mentioned in this list. Otherwise, this chapter would share the fate of the *Epistle to Egbert* if the writer had treated of all the subjects he had in his mind—it would be extended to an immoderate length. We shall here consider two of the prelates who figure most prominently in the correspondence, viz. Daniel of Winchester and Egbert of York.

Daniel, bishop of Winchester.—On the division of the West-Saxon diocese (A.D. 705), Daniel was made bishop of Winchester. Bede testifies to his knowledge of Holy Scripture.[1] He also testifies that it was Daniel, " the most reverend bishop of the West-Saxons," who imparted to himself some information about the

---

[1] H.E. v. 18. A later bishop of Winchester—Cyneheard—speaks of him as " doctissimus Dei plebis famulus " (Mon. Mog. p. 269).

ecclesiastical history of Wessex, Sussex, and the Isle
of Wight.[1]

Towards the end of the seventh century, a mission
had been established by the Northumbrian Willibrord
in Frisia. It was crowned with a considerable degree
of success, although a formidable obstacle to the
spread of Christianity always existed so long as the
pagan king Rathbod ("the enemy of the Catholic
Church," as the abbess Bugge describes him in one
of her letters [2]) was alive.[3] Boniface set forth from the
monastery of Nursling, and attempted to work in
Frisia, but he found himself obliged to return to England. Paganism had again lifted up its head in the
district which had been evangelised by Willibrord.
Rathbod had succeeded in gaining the ascendancy
over the part of Frisia which had formerly been under
Frankish rule, a persecution of Christians ensued, and
there was a relapse into idolatry. Fresh missionary
enterprise at this juncture was impossible. But
Boniface's task was only abandoned for a time. The
hope was entertained of returning some day, if a way
were opened up, and of preaching the Gospel in these
parts.[4] On setting out a second time, he received a
commendatory letter from his own bishop, Daniel.[5]

---

[1] H.E. Pref.   [2] Mon. Mog. p. 75.

[3] Much interesting information about Rathbod will be found in
Alcuin, *Vita S. Willibrordi*, cc. 5, 9, 10, 11, 13. He died in A.D. 719.

[4] He had to leave fields which his biographer, speaking in a figurative
sense, says were dry and still in need of the blessing of heavenly dew.
Vita Bonf. c. 4.

[5] Mon. Mog. pp, 61–62 ; H. & S. iii. 302.

The writer speaks of the virtue of hospitality to travellers, and adduces the stories of Abraham and of Lot by way of illustration. He commends the bearer of the letter to the good offices of kings, dukes, bishops, abbots, presbyters, and " spiritual sons signed with the Name of Christ."

We have a remarkable letter from Daniel to Boniface with regard to methods of winning pagans to Christ.[1] Questions were to be asked regarding the generation of the pagan deities, and such-like topics. We may doubt the wisdom of this method, but Daniel is careful to point out that it was to be used in a spirit of moderation, and not with a view to insult or irritate the hearers. Pagan superstitions were to be compared with Christian dogmas. Use was also to be made of the fact that *temporal* advantages were on the side of the Christians, who were in possession of fertile lands, whilst the pagans were in possession of lands held in the grip of cold. This fact, together with the overthrow of idolatry almost all over the world by the advance of Christianity, was to be taken as showing the impotence and injustice of the pagan deities.

At the end of the letter, we have a touching allusion to Daniel's ill-health. He was " weighed down by bodily weakness." But he strove to be enabled, like the Psalmist, to recognise the just judgment and affliction of God. He begged the prayers of Boniface and his companions, so that the Lord would have

[1] Mon. Mog. pp. 71–74 ; H. & S. iii. 304–306.

mercy upon him and enable him to sing, " according to the multitude of my griefs in my heart are Thy consolations, O Lord, they have rejoiced my soul."

We pass on to another letter. Boniface, trusting in " the proved wisdom and friendship " of Daniel, seeks his advice with regard to a matter which had been troubling him greatly.[1] In his oath to the Papacy, he had sworn " to have no communion or fellowship " with any bishops who were known to him " to live contrary to the ancient decrees of the Holy Fathers." [2] In actual practice, however, he had found it impossible literally to carry out this part of his oath. The support of the Frankish temporal power was necessary to him, as he himself explains, for the successful prosecution of his work. So from time to time he had to visit the Frankish court. It was impossible for him on such occasions to avoid the bodily fellowship of " false priests and hypocrites." This circumstance caused him much searching of heart, as he conceived that such intercourse—unless he could bring the others to amendment—was contrary to the promise he had made in his oath to the Papacy. He longed to get counsel from Daniel which would enable a " sad and doubting son " to know what to do.[3] In this same

[1] Mon. Mog. pp. 157-161 ; H. & S. iii. 343-346.
[2] Mon. Mog. p. 77.
[3] It seems somewhat strange that Boniface should have been troubled in mind so much on this matter. One would have thought that his scruples would have been set at rest by the common-sense advice once given to him in a letter from Pope Gregory II. (Mon. Mog. pp. 90-91).

letter, he makes a request for a book written by Winbert, abbot of Nursling,[1] and he mentions presents that he is sending to Daniel.[2] The letter concludes with spiritual consolation to the bishop, who had now been afflicted with blindness, and with a request for his prayers. The beauty of the language in which the consolation is expressed, and the comfort of the thoughts, are both very noticeable.

To the above letter Daniel sent a reply.[3] He seeks to remove his friend's scruples. It was impossible for Boniface to avoid the communion of " false brethren or priests " unless he went out of the world altogether, because such persons were found everywhere and always. S. Paul had this experience. Other Christian pioneers testified that they had suffered the same thing, or that posterity would have to suffer it. After various references to Holy Scripture and to the Fathers, with regard to the mingling of good and bad in this world, he speaks of " simulation," setting forth views which he says he had taken " from the works of ancient doctors." In connection with Scriptural instances of " simulation," we find an amazing piece of exegesis. He is speaking of the case of Jacob, who covered himself with goat-skins. " He did this in order that he might be thought to be some one that he was not ; and, if the matter is diligently and faithfully considered, it is not a lie, but a mystery. By goat-skins are signified

---

[1] V. inf. p. 61.   [2] V. inf. pp. 107–108.
[3] Mon. Mog. pp. 161–166.

sins, by him who covered himself with them He is signified Who bears the sins of others."

Daniel gratefully acknowledges Boniface's consolations, and he ends his letter with a beautiful passage. Though he and his friend are separated from one another by a great distance both of land and sea, " yet we are bowed down by a like burden of tribulations. The working of Satan is the same here and there." Earnestly he begs that Boniface and he may strengthen each other by a mutual bond of prayer.

It may hardly be worth while to make mention of a vision of the lower world in which some one saw " a sad and wailing and numerous company of infants who died without Baptism, especially under bishop Daniel." [1] If there be any truth at all in this charge, we might infer that the failure to have these infants baptised was due to carelessness on the bishop's part. Possibly, however, they were children of pagan parents whom he was unable to reach. His ill-health and blindness would interfere with his episcopal activities. He resigned his see in A.D. 744, and died in the following year.

Egbert, bishop (afterwards archbishop) of York.—This prelate, a brother of Eadbert, king of Northumbria, succeeded Wilfrid II. (who resigned his see) in A.D. 732. We are told that he was the first bishop of York, since the days of Paulinus, who received the pall from the Pope. [2] A highly laudatory account of him is con-

[1] Mon. Mog. p. 276.   [2] S.D. p. 13.

tained in Alcuin's well-known poem.[1] The joint
rule of the two brothers—king and archbishop—when
one helped the other, is represented as having been a
happy time for the Northumbrian people.

The two letters which Egbert received from Boniface
reveal the York prelate as a man of literary tastes.[2]
This agrees with what we read of him elsewhere. It is
stated that he was a pupil of Bede, and we see that he
became a notable teacher himself, having Alcuin as
one of his pupils.[3] He is described as being, during
his tenure of the see at York, *egregius doctor*.[4] Bede had
enjoyed literary fellowship with him on a visit to York,
and there was hope that the visit might be repeated
in the following year.[5]

Egbert and Boniface stood on common ground with
regard to their love of learning. Egbert had sent
books, for which the recipient was most grateful.
A request is made in the first letter for works of Bede.
These works are not specified by name, but the author
is praised, and it is requested that " we also may enjoy
the candle which the Lord has given to you." In
the second letter, a more specific request is made.
The simile of a shining candle is again employed, and
Bede is described as a " spiritual presbyter and investi-
gator of the Holy Scriptures." With a view to

---

[1] *De Pontif. Ebor.* 1247 ff.
[2] Mon. Mog. pp. 178–180, 249–251.
[3] *Vita Alch.* c. 2, where we read of the subjects taught, and of the teacher's methods. The teacher was a man of prayer.
[4] *De Pontif. Ebor.* 1259.   [5] *Ep. ad Egb.* § 1.

usefulness in the work of preaching, the writer was specially eager to have Bede's *Homilies* and his commentary on the Proverbs of Solomon. But the literary presents were not all on one side. Boniface sends copies made by himself in the archives of the Roman Church of some of S. Gregory's *Epistles*.

Boniface does not treat merely of literary matters in his letters to Egbert. *E.g.* he alludes to the solemn warning sent by himself and other bishops to Ethelbald, king of Mercia.[1] It would seem that this letter had first been sent to Egbert for revision. That prelate is exhorted, if he saw any signs of germination in Northumbria of the evils described, to cut them down and root them up. " It is," the writer says, " an evil unheard-of in past ages, and—as servants of God here who are learned in the Scriptures say—threefold or fourfold exceeding the wantonness of the Sodomites : that a Christian nation, contrary to the custom of the whole earth, yea, contrary to the commandment of God, should despise lawful marriage, give itself up to incest, wantonness, and adultery, and wickedly violate women who are consecrated and who have taken the veil." [2]

There are other points in the correspondence of Boniface and Lullus with their English episcopal friends on which we should here like to dwell—*e.g.* the interest taken in the missionary work, and the joy felt over its progress, as set forth in a letter from Torthelm to

[1] *V. sup.* p. 2.   [2] Mon. Mog. p. 180.

E

Boniface [1] ; the beautiful thoughts on the death of that missionary, expressed in a letter from Milred to Lullus [2] ; the short letter in which Cyneheard assures Lullus of his prayers. [3] It is well, in view of possibly exaggerated ideas which may prevail as to the decline of English religious life in the eighth century, to have these definite instances of episcopal piety before us. The piety does not strike us as consisting merely in the use of conventional and formal phrases ; there is an appearance of spontaneity about it.

At this point, it may be helpful to glance at the Council of Clovesho, and especially to notice the high standard which was set before the episcopate in the opening canons. [4] This famous Council was held in the days when Cuthbert was archbishop of Canterbury. Many prelates were present—Canterbury, Rochester, Lichfield, Leicester, Hereford, Winchester, Sherborne, Dunwich, London, Worcester, Lindsey, Selsey. Ethelbald, king of Mercia, was also present, together with his leading men. A letter was read from Pope Zacharias, and was interpreted into English. The first canon warns bishops against carelessness in living, slackness in teaching, absorption in secular business. The second canon reminds them that they are " ministers of one Lord, and fellow-servants in one ministry." It goes on to remind them that " though they are separated in sees in different places, yet they

---

[1] Mon. Mog. p. 252.   [2] Ibid. p. 267.
[3] Ibid. p. 287.   [4] H. & S. iii. 363-364.

are joined together in mind in one spirit, that they should serve God in faith, hope, and charity, praying diligently for one another, that each one may be able faithfully to finish the course of his conflict." The third canon enjoins thorough visitation of dioceses once a year, the calling together of people of both sexes and various grades of society to suitable places, so that teaching may be given to them, especially in the case of those " who seldom hear the Word of God."

We shall now briefly consider Egbert's successors in the see of York, and shall take our material mainly from Alcuin's correspondence.

(a) *Albert* (=Ethelbert=Cena). One of the most valuable portions of Alcuin's poem on the Prelates and Saints of the Church of York is that in which he describes Albert (who was a kinsman of Egbert), and tells us about the contents of the York library.[1] Albert was " mente sagax, non ore loquax." He was especially noted as a scholar and a teacher, and was an indefatigable collector of books, in search of which he travelled overseas. We have a beautiful picture of him and of his pupils as they studied S. John's Gospel together.[2] Alcuin speaks of him as " my beloved master." [3] Ultimately, he resigned the archbishopric, and lived in retirement till his death.

We have two letters which passed between Lullus and Albert.[4] The York prelate is asked to send one of

---

[1] *De Pontif. Ebor.* 1395 ff.
[2] *Vita Alch.* c.
[3] Mon. Alc. p. 331.
[4] Mon. Mog. pp. 288, 290–291.

the books put forth by " the presbyter Bede of blessed memory." The choice was to lie between four books on 1 Samuel (to the death of Saul), three books on Esdras and Nehemiah, four books on S. Mark's Gospel.

(*b*) *Eanbald I.* This prelate figured prominently in Alcuin's life. They had been fellow-students under Albert.[1] It was at Eanbald's command that Alcuin went to Rome to fetch the pall for the new archbishop, and it was on his way back that his momentous meeting with King Charles took place at Parma.[2]

From one of Alcuin's letters, it would appear that at one time there was a possibility of the archbishop resigning his see.[3] In another letter,[4] Alcuin points out that the Church of York has hitherto been free from simony in the election to the archbishopric. The sin of simony, he declares, is of the most heinous kind. " He who sells a bishopric will receive gold, but he will lose the kingdom of God." Christ and the Church, he points out, are one body.

It is evident that the news of Eanbald's death affected his old friend very much.[5] " He was to me a father and a brother and a most faithful friend." [6]

---

[1] Mon. Alc. p. 324.
[2] *Vita Alch.* c. 6. We learn (*ibid.* l.c.) that this was not the first occasion on which they had met.
[3] Mon. Alc. pp. 256–257.
[4] *Ibid.* pp. 257–258.
[5] It is a remarkable fact that Eanbald I., Ethelred (king of Northumbria), Offa (king of Mercia), Egferth (king of Mercia), all died in the same year (796).
[6] Mon. Alc. p. 324.

(c) *Eanbald II.* Details are given by Symeon of Durham with regard to the burial of Eanbald I. and the consecration of his successor.[1] Alcuin alludes to the fact that Eanbald II. had been one of his old pupils.[2] We have three letters written by him to the new Primate.[3] They show that Eanbald had been an obedient and a beloved pupil.[4] They also show that he did not enjoy robust health.[5] Testimony is given to his " nobility of mind, and his integrity in the Holy Faith.",[6] He was certainly overwhelmed by his old master with much good counsel. A high conception of the episcopal office was set before him in these three letters.[7]

Alcuin is very emphatic about the national degeneracy towards the close of the century. " There are times of tribulation everywhere in our land. Faith is departing, truth does not speak, wickedness is growing, and arrogance is adding itself to our miseries." [8] He laments the decline of preaching. " Now, through our sins, labourers are few in the harvest of the Lord." [9] Doubtless, the archbishops

---

[1] S.D. p. 34.   [2] Mon. Alc. pp. 331, 337.
[3] *Ibid.* pp. 331–339.
[4] *Ibid.* pp. 331–332.
[5] *Ibid.* p. 332. Cf. *ibid.* p. 254.
[6] *Ibid.* pp. 337–338.
[7] Emissaries came from York to Rome to beg the pall for the new prelate. Alcuin writes to the Pope (Leo III.) and asks him to grant their request. " In those parts," he adds, " the authority of the sacred pall is highly necessary in order to crush the perversity of wicked men and to preserve the authority of Holy Church." *Ibid.* p. 359.
[8] *Ibid.* p. 349.   [9] *Ibid.* p. 518.

and bishops must bear a share of the blame. But our brief survey of the English episcopate in this century will have failed in one of its objects if it does not show that there were archbishops and bishops who had the interests of religion and of learning at heart.[1]

[1] There were seven persons altogether who occupied the see of York in the eighth century—Bosa, John, Wilfrid II., Egbert, Albert, Eanbald I., Eanbald II. Where York is concerned, Alcuin perhaps is a somewhat partial witness. But, from what he tells us (in his *De Pontif. Ebor.* and in his letters) about the above-mentioned prelates, it would seem that *all* of them were men of high personal character. On the earlier prelates in this list, cf. H.E. v. 2, 3, 6, 20.

CHAPTER IV

MONASTIC LIFE

ONE of the greatest scandals in connection with eighth-century monastic life has been touched upon in the previous chapter, viz. the existence of many establishments in Northumbria which were called monasteries, but which were utterly unworthy of that name. Bede devotes a large part of his *Epistle to Egbert* to a consideration of this subject, and to remedies which he proposed.[1] The trouble began after the death of King Aldfrid. Laymen, on the pretext of founding monasteries, would obtain a grant of land—for which they paid money—and the land so granted was made, by royal decree, a hereditary possession. Attestations were given both by ecclesiastical and secular authorities. The grantees would then gather together a motley crowd, consisting of any of their own retainers whom they could persuade to receive the tonsure, of vagabond monks expelled from monasteries, and of monks whom they could draw away. The strange spectacle was seen of laymen presiding, under the rôle of abbots, over so-called monasteries, although these laymen at

[1] *Ep. ad Egb.* §§ 10–14.

55

the same time might be royal thanes or reeves. Of the internal character of these establishments, little need be said. The so-called abbots were "free from Divine and human service, serving only their own lusts." No true monastic life was observed, but there was scope for wantonness, vanity, and intemperance.

Of the national danger involved in the foundation of so many of these false monasteries, Bede was fully aware. The State had been denuded of many persons who should have been its defenders in the event of invasion by barbarians. So much land had been given away that it was impossible to provide settlements for sons of noblemen or of soldiers who had served in war. Also, it was rendered difficult to find vacant places for the creation of episcopal sees.

The bishops are blamed, to some extent, for the deplorable state of affairs. They had subscribed the deeds by which the lands were conveyed, and they did not seem to show any special eagerness to have their subscriptions revoked. Bede himself thinks that some of these false monasteries might well be appropriated, if revenue were needed for the new bishoprics which he so strongly advocated. He also impresses upon Egbert the need of episcopal visitation of monasteries. "It is your duty," he says, "most diligently to see what is done rightly, what is done wrongly, in the several monasteries of your diocese." And again, "It is your duty, I say, to take steps, so that in places consecrated to God the devil does not gain the rule ;

so that a position is not won for discord instead of peace, for quarrels instead of piety, for drunkenness instead of sobriety, for fornications and homicides instead of charity and chastity."

Similarly, in the twentieth canon of the Council of Clovesho, bishops are exhorted to see that monasteries deserve their name, that they are not the abodes of poets, harpers, musicians, and buffoons, but of persons who pray, read, and praise God.[1]

Mention has been made already of a despondent letter written to Boniface by the abbess Eangyth and her daughter.[2] Allusion is made in it to some of the difficulties of monastic life.[3] We are not told the name of the monastery in question ; but, from the reference which we find to the presence of persons of both sexes and of different ages, we see that it must have been a " double " monastery. The writers were evidently very dissatisfied. They speak of domestic difficulty and of strife. They attribute this discord to the Evil One, who sows this kind of trouble everywhere, but especially in monasteries. Then they go on to speak of poverty, bewailing the narrow extent of the monastic estate. These two troubles—internal discord and limited revenue—are curiously reminiscent of what may so often be read in medieval monastic history. The third trouble was royal opposition, which had been brought about by the accusations of ill-wishers.

[1] H. & S. iii. 369.   [2] V. sup. p. 34.
[3] Mon. Mog. pp. 67-68.

The particular form in which royal disfavour was shown is not mentioned. Lastly, anxiety was caused by the service expected on the part of the king and queen, the bishop, the reeve, etc. This last anxiety was probably of a financial nature, and would certainly press heavily on an impoverished community.[1]

We find instances of monastic troubles caused by the interference of the secular power. Boniface and other bishops allude to the report that Ethelbald, king of Mercia, had violated " many privileges of churches and monasteries." [2] They also allude to the report that the royal reeves and thanes violently exacted greater service from monks and priests than had been previously done by Christian kings. Commenting on this report, the writers state that from the time when the English people were converted to the true God by means of the preachers of the Catholic Faith who were sent by S. Gregory, " the privileges of churches in the English realm remained uninjured and unbroken down to the times of Ceolred, king of the Mercians, and of Osred, king of the Deirans and the Bernicians." [3] Similarly, in a letter from Boniface to Cuthbert, archbishop of Canterbury, allusion is made to the sin of violent seizure of monasteries by laymen. In a sense, the passage is almost an echo of Bede's complaint Boniface says : " That a layman, whether an emperor, or a king, or one of the reeves or thanes, supported by secular power, should violently seize for himself a

[1] Cf. H. & S. iii. 239.   [2] Mon. Mog. p. 174.   [3] Ibid. l.c.

monastery from the power of bishop, abbot, or abbess, and should himself begin to rule in place of the abbot, and have monks under him, and possess money which was won by the Blood of Christ ; such a man the ancient Fathers styled a robber, a sacrilegious person, a slayer of the poor, a wolf of the devil entering into the fold of Christ, and one to be condemned with the greatest bond of anathema before the tribunal of Christ." [1] In the same letter, there is an allusion to the forced labour of monks on royal buildings, " a thing which is not heard of as having been done in the whole of Christendom, save only among the people of England." [2]

We have a letter written by Pope Paul I., in which he exhorts Eadbert, king of Northumbria, to restore to an abbot named Forthred three monasteries violently taken from him by that king, and given to a patrician named Moll, the abbot's brother. [3]

It is not surprising that the desire for " the quiet of a contemplative life " caused the abbess Bugge to give up the cares of a monastery, although it would seem that she afterwards resumed them. [4] Still, as in the seventh century, we find high-born women undertaking the work of monastic government. We read of at least two widowed queens—Edilthyde, wife of Ethelwald, king of Northumbria ; and Cynethrith, wife of Offa,

---

[1] Mon. Mog. pp. 208-209.   [2] *Ibid.* p. 210.
[3] H. & S. iii. 394-395.
[4] Mon. Mog. pp. 233, 236, 254.

king of Mercia—who became abbesses.[1] Alcuin
advised that Ethelfleda (the widowed queen of
Ethelred) should go into a monastery.[2]

That there were grave irregularities disfiguring
monastic life in this century is only too clear. We read
of unchastity among nuns in the days of Osred and of
Ceolred.[3] There was a similar report in the days of
Ethelbald.[4] In the flood of immorality which,
according to Alcuin, had swept over the land at a
later date, some nuns were engulfed.[5] The bonds of
monastic discipline towards the end of the century
must have been much relaxed, when the same writer
tells us that " the servants of God throughout the
monasteries live more after the manner of laymen than
of monks." [6] He gives repeated warnings against
gluttony, drunkenness, vanity in dress, and neglect of
study. To what extent some of these evils then
prevailed in English monasteries, it is impossible to
say. But the mere fact that he should have warned
his readers so insistently on these topics shows that he
himself considered there was need of warning.

On the monastic neglect of study, we can speak
more or less definitely. It is true, there are some
bright spots. The monastery of Nursling, in the days
when Winfrid (Boniface) was teaching there, would
seem to have been a hive of literary industry. The

---

[1] Mon. Alc. pp. 274, n. 1, 292, n. 4.　　　[2] *Ibid.* p. 294.
[3] Mon. Mog. pp. 174-175.　　　　　　　　[4] *Ibid.* p. 170.
[5] Mon. Alc. p. 181.　　　　　　　　　　　　[6] *Ibid.* p. 373.

fame of the new teacher was noised abroad, and many persons flocked to him for instruction.[1] Abbot Winbert must have taken pains in compiling a book on six of the Prophets.[2] Boniface was especially eager to get this book, and asks Daniel to send it. It was written in clear and separate characters, very different from the small and connected characters which Boniface, owing to failing eyesight, found so difficult to read. Eadburga, abbess of S. Mildred, Thanet, was in the habit of sending books to that missionary. She was asked on one occasion to have the Epistles of S. Peter written out for him in letters of gold.[3] A peculiarly interesting passage, as showing the difficulties under which the labour of monastic copyists was sometimes carried on, occurs in a letter from Guthbert, abbot of Wearmouth and Jarrow, to Lullus.[4] The abbot had himself been a pupil of Bede (*ad pedes ejus nutritus*), and was asked to send some of his master's works. He and his boys had done their best to comply with this request, and had prepared the *Lives of Cuthbert*, one in prose, one in verse. He would gladly have done more if he could, but the winter had been so severe, accompanied by frost, cold, wind, and rain, that " the hand of the writer was hindered from copying many books." [5]

The above instances will have shown that monastic

[1] *Vita Bonf.* c. 2.   [2] Mon. Mog. p. 160.
[3] *Ibid.* p. 99.   [4] *Ibid.* pp. 300–302.
[5] Perhaps this was the severe winter referred to in S.D. p. 21.

learning and literary industry had not altogether died
out. But, on the whole, the picture is a dark one.
Bede speaks of monks who were ignorant of Latin.[1]
Alcuin, writing to the monks of Wearmouth and
Jarrow, says : " Let the Rule of S. Benedict be often
read in the assembly of the brethren and expounded in
your own tongue, so that it may be understood by all." [2]
The seventh canon of the Council of Clovesho had
borne testimony to the general decline of monastic
study.[3] " Sad to relate, in these times very few
persons are found who in their inmost heart are carried
away with a love of sacred knowledge." The want of
application in study is pointed out, and mention is
made of other pursuits which had a greater attraction.
An exhortation is given that boys should be trained in
schools, with a view to the love of sacred knowledge,
and so fitted to render service to the Church of God.
We might, however, have expected better things at
Wearmouth and Jarrow. It was a community with
great traditions. The monks are exhorted by Alcuin.
" Call to mind," he says, " what noble fathers you had,
and be not unworthy sons of such great progenitors." [4]

[1] *Ep. ad Egb.* § 5.
[2] Mon. Alc. p. 198. It can hardly be inferred from the above passage
that the Rule of S. Benedict, pure and simple, was followed at Wearmouth and Jarrow. Earlier in the letter, Alcuin urges that the
observances laid down by Benedict Biscop and Ceolfrid should be
followed. The Rule which Benedict Biscop drew up was of a conflate
character. See *C.Q.R.*, Oct. 1928, p. 74.
   On Wilfrid and the Rule of S. Benedict, see Eddius, cc. 14, 47.
[3] H. & S. iii. 364–365.
[4] Mon. Alc. p. 199.

This was the community which possessed the "most noble and most copious library" associated with the names of Benedict Biscop and of Ceolfrid.[1] Alcuin evidently alludes to this library when he exhorts his readers "to look at the treasures of books."[2] But it would seem that among the younger members, at least, there was a disinclination for study. Boys were exhorted to accustom themselves "to join in the praises of the Heavenly King, not to dig out the holes of foxes, not to follow the swift courses of hares . . . let boys learn the Holy Scriptures, so that, when the due age comes, they may be able to teach others. *Qui non discit in pueritia, non docet in senectute.*" Bede's zeal for study in his youth was to be remembered. He now has praise from men, and a glorious reward with God. "By his example, then, rouse the sleeping minds. Sit at the feet of masters, open books, examine letters, understand their meaning."[3]

Although Alcuin addressed solemn warnings, *more suo*, to the monks of Wearmouth and Jarrow, it would not seem that he was altogether dissatisfied with the state of affairs in that community. We have a letter from him to "the most holy brethren who serve God in the church of S. Peter"[4] (probably the one at Wearmouth[5]). He states that the place of the monks' habitation was "very desirable" to himself. He

[1] H.A.B. §§ 11, 15.   [2] Mon. Alc. p. 199.   [3] *Ibid.* pp. 199-200.
[4] *Ibid.* pp. 843-845 ; H. & S. iii. 470-471.
[5] H. & S. iii. 471, *n.* b.

alludes to a personal visit which he had paid, and to the satisfaction afforded to him by what he then saw. It is in this letter that he tells the anecdote about Bede and angelic visits at the Canonical Hours.[1] " It is told that our master and your patron, the blessed Bede, said : I know that angels visit the Canonical Hours and the assemblies of the brethren. What if they do not find me there among the brethren ? Will they not say, Where is Bede ? Why does he not come to the appointed prayers with the brethren ? " A comparison is made immediately afterwards between the cenobitic and the anchoretic life. " It is much better to pray, eat, and sleep in common with the brethren than with danger to remain alone in a special habitation."

A few more letters, bearing on the famous community at Wearmouth and Jarrow, may be noticed :

(1) Ceolfrid had been a loyal friend and helper to Benedict Biscop. For many years he held the abbacy, but ultimately he determined to resign and

---

[1] Alcuin would seem to be alluding to this anecdote when he urges his friends at York not to be absent from the Services of the Canonical Hours (Mon. Alc. p. 253). We are told that he himself, in his earlier years, was often in the habit of attending these Services in daytime, but very rarely at night-time. We are also told that he was a lover of Virgil more than of the Psalms (*Vita Alch.* c. 1). In his old age, however, we read that he could never be satiated with the chanting of Psalms (*ibid.* c. 8). He no longer wished to hear what his biographer calls the " lies " of Virgil, nor did he wish his disciples to read them (*ibid. c.* 10). On Bede's attitude to Virgil and other classical writers, see Plummer, *Baedae Op. Hist.* Introd. liii.

to go on pilgrimage to Rome. After a farewell scene of almost unparalleled solemnity, he set forth. Shortly after his departure, a new abbot was elected. The choice fell on Hwaetbert, of whose attainments and previous work Bede speaks in high terms.[1] The new abbot took with him some of the brethren, and followed after Ceolfrid, who was waiting for a ship to take him overseas. The old abbot rejoiced to hear of the election, which he confirmed. Before setting sail from the Humber, he received from his successor a letter of commendation to Pope Gregory II. The early part has been preserved to us.[2]

It is an interesting letter. Hwaetbert describes himself as " abbot of the monastery of the most blessed Peter, chief of the Apostles, in *Saxony*." He alludes to Ceolfrid's long tenure of office—more than forty years. It does not, however, seem altogether tactful to speak of the bearer—to whom, we are told, he had read the letter [3]—as being now " worn out with old age," and as " likely soon to die." (But the bearer himself thought death was near.) The conviction is expressed in the letter that Ceolfrid will be an intercessor and a protector in the Heavenly Realm.

Ceolfrid had been to Rome before.[4] But on this occasion he never reached that city, as he died at Langres (in Burgundy) a few months after he had

---

[1] H.A.B. § 18, where we are told that Hwaetbert had once stayed for a considerable time in Rome. It was at his request that Bede wrote the commentary on the Apocalypse. Migne, *P.L.* xciv. 692.

[2] H.A.A. § 30 ; H.A.B. § 19.   [3] H.A.A. § 29.   [4] *Ibid.* § 10.

started on his pilgrimage. So passed away one of the brightest ornaments of English monasticism.

(2) The interesting fact is revealed that Alcuin's name had been placed in the Liber Albus of the community, so that " he was one of them, wherever, by God's will, he might be." [1]

(3) Alcuin exhorts a newly-appointed abbot to live " after the examples of the holy fathers Benedict and Ceolfrid," and he reminds him " how quickly those were cut off from this life who in any small particle broke the statutes of the first parents." [2]

(4) We have a letter of a most delightful kind, written by abbot Guthbert to Lullus. [3] It may be called a human document, and helps us to understand what manner of man the abbot was. He praises Bede, and his testimony is of peculiar value, because, as we noticed earlier in the chapter, he had been one of Bede's pupils. " It seems right to me," says the abbot, " that the whole English people in all provinces, wherever they have been found, should return thanks to God, because He has given them in their own nation so marvellous a man, endowed with diverse gifts, and one who was so careful to exercise his gifts, and who likewise lived in good conversation. By experience, having been brought up at his feet, I have learned this which I tell."

---

[1] Mon. Alc. p. 839. For an evident allusion to this fact, cf. *ibid.* p. 201. From *Vita Cutb.* (Pref.), we learn of an order being given for Bede's name to be placed in the Liber Albus of the community at Lindisfarne.

[2] Mon. Alc. pp. 841–842.   [3] Mon. Mog. pp. 300–302.

Lullus had sent a silken covering for the relics of Bede. It is somewhat touching to read what Guthbert did with a variegated covering which had been sent as a protection for his own body against the cold. " I gave it with great joy to Almighty God and to the blessed Apostle Paul, for a covering of the altar which was consecrated to God in his church ; because I have lived under his protection in this monastery for forty-six years."

The heroic efforts to cope with the transcription of Bede's works, in spite of the winter cold, have been already noted.[1] At the end of the letter he promises, if his life is spared, to do what Lullus wishes in this matter. He alludes to presents which he had despatched by a presbyter named Hunwini, who died on the way to Rome, so he did not know if these presents had been duly delivered or not. He was now sending other presents.[2]

His interest in art and in music is shown by requests which he made. One of these requests was for workers in glass. " If there is any man in your diocese who has skill in making vessels of glass, I beg that you will send him to me when there is a suitable occasion." If such a person could not be found within the limits of Lullus's diocese, but could be found elsewhere, his friend is asked to use persuasion to make him come to England. He then adds, " of this same art we are ignorant and destitute." It seems somewhat strange

[1] *V. sup.* p. 61.   [2] *V. inf.* p. 109

that it should have been so. Wilfrid, in the previous century, had caused glass to be put in the windows of the church at York.[1]   Benedict Biscop, in connection with the building of the monastic church at Wearmouth, had procured makers of glass from Gaul, and these foreign artificers had taught the art to the English people.[2]

It is by means of letters such as the above that we are enabled to get vivid pictures of contemporary life, and to understand something of the *personalities* of actors in the drama.

To sum up.   In the seventh century, in the days of Oswy and of Egfrid, monasticism flourished in the North.   But even then, in view of what we read about Coldingham,[3] we must beware of painting too roseate a picture.   In the eighth century there was probably a gradual deterioration.   It is ominous and significant that Wilfrid should have thought it necessary to leave money to the heads of two of his monasteries, with a view to purchasing the friendship of kings and bishops.[4] The traditions of the saintly founder of Wearmouth and Jarrow would not be forgotten in the days when Ceolfrid and Hwaetbert were abbots.[5]   Nor would the cause of learning suffer while Albinus was in charge of the Kentish monastery of SS. Peter and Paul.   We see a spirit of affection and respect expressed for him in the letter prefixed to Bede's *Ecclesiastical History*.

[1] Eddius, c. 16.   [2] H.A.B. § 5.   [3] H.E. iv. 25.
[4] Eddius, c. 63.   [5] H.A.B. §§ 15-20.

The same spirit appears in the Preface, where Bede's great indebtedness is expressed to that abbot, who is stated to have been " before all, the author and helper of this work." In the text itself, eloquent testimony is paid to the learning of Albinus, who is described as having no small knowledge of Greek, and as being just as familiar with Latin as with his own tongue.[1]

As the century wore on, monastic life must sometimes have been extraordinarily difficult, in view of the unsettled state of the country, the political dissensions and violence which so often prevailed. To crown all, the raids of the Northmen began. In A.D. 793, the sack of Lindisfarne took place. Jarrow suffered in the following year. It was impossible to know, with such a dark shadow hanging over the land, where the next blow might fall. The fear of impending danger would have its effect on monastic life, and would be an obstacle in the way of strict enforcement of discipline and of whole-hearted devotion to study.[2] Alcuin's exhortations were wholesome, but they were also difficult of fulfilment.

[1] H.E. v. 20.
[2] How far the enforcement of monastic rule would have been possible in Northumbria during the closing years of the eighth century is a question which may be left to the reader of Symeon of Durham to decide.

CHAPTER V

DOCTRINE AND DEVOTION

WE find nothing in England corresponding to the extravagances of Aldebert and Clemens, who were condemned in a Roman synod (A.D. 745).[1] Towards the end of the century, Western Christendom was agitated by the Adoptionist heresy, associated with the names of Elipandus and of Felix.[2] King Charles and Alcuin were much concerned in the controversy.[3] A Council was held at Frankfort (A.D. 794), and it is noticeable that representatives *de Britanniae partibus* were present.[4] Adoptionism was condemned. A year or two previously, we are told by Symeon of Durham that King Charles sent to Britain a synodal book which had been sent to himself from Constantinople. There were many things in this book which were " inconsistent with and contrary to the true faith," especially the almost unanimous decision of the Nicene Council (A.D. 787) with regard to the worship of Images. This

---

[1] Mon. Mog. pp. 132–133, 136 ff.   [2] *Vita Alch.* c. 7.

[3] Mon. Alc. pp. 18–19, 255. Alcuin laments that many people were presuming to do what the soldiers at the Cross did not dare to do, viz. to rend the seamless robe of Christ.

[4] H. & S. iii. 481.

was a thing which "the Church of God altogether abhors." [1] The action of that Council was likewise condemned at Frankfort. [2]

A Northumbrian synod, presided over by Eanbald II., archbishop of York, was held towards the end of the century. The place of meeting was Pincanhalh. [3] The persons who were present professed the orthodoxy of their Faith. They confirmed the decisions of the first Five Councils. Having done so, they returned home, " praising God for all His benefits." [4]

Contemporary letters tell us much about Holy Scripture, Prayer (both for the living and for the departed), the Sacraments, etc. We now proceed to a consideration of these subjects.

(i) HOLY SCRIPTURE

We cannot read these letters without being impressed (*e.g.* in a consolatory letter written to the abbess Bugge by Boniface [5]) by the wonderful knowledge which the writers sometimes show of Holy Scripture, and by the aptness of the quotations which they make. Of the high estimation in which Holy Scripture was held, and of the importance attached to its study, illustrations abound.

[1] S.D. p. 30.
[2] H. & S. iii. 481-482. Cf. *ibid.* iii. 469, *n.* a.
[3] Generally identified with Finchale, Co. Durham.
[4] S.D. pp. 35-36.
[5] Mon. Mog. pp. 233-234.

(1) Bede urges Egbert to study Holy Scripture, and especially to read S. Paul's Epistles to Timothy and to Titus.[1] Egbert is also urged to read Gregory's *Pastoral* and *Homilies*.[2]

(2) Boniface, in the earlier part of his life, writes to a young man named Nithardus.[3] He urges upon him the study of Holy Scripture, and quotes various Old Testament passages regarding meditation on God's Law. Such study is the means of acquiring Divine wisdom, " which is more splendid than gold, more beautiful than silver, brighter than a carbuncle, clearer than crystal, more precious than a topaz." He himself, if he has the opportunity, will do his best to help Nithardus in this study.

(3) Boniface thanks the abbess Eadburga for her gifts of Sacred Books. She has " brought the consolation of spiritual light to an exile in Germany." One who is seeking to throw light into the " dark corners " of that country will fall into the snare of death, " unless he has the Word of the Lord as a lantern to his feet

---

[1] *Ep. ad Egb.* § 3.

[2] *Ibid.* l.c. We may note other instances in which Gregory's *Pastoral* is recommended. Boniface refers to it in a letter which he wrote to Cuthbert, archbishop of Canterbury (Mon. Mog. p. 208). Alcuin writes to Eanbald II. : " Wherever you go, let the *Pastoral Book* of S. Gregory go with you. Read and re-read it many a time . . . it is a mirror of the pontifical life, and a medicine against the several wounds caused by the fraud of the devil " (Mon. Alc. p. 339. Cf. H. & S. iii. 505, *n.* b). Similar advice is given by Alcuin to " a very holy brother and a very dear son," who was a bishop, addressed under the name of Speratus (Mon. Alc. p. 355).

[3] Mon. Mog. pp. 50–53.

and a light to his path." [1] It was this same abbess who, on another occasion, was asked to have the Epistles of S. Peter written out in letters of gold.[2]

(4) A letter is written by Boniface to a friend of his youth, an abbot named Duddo, who seems to have been an old pupil.[3] Duddo's help is asked in the study of Holy Scripture, and he is requested to send part of a tractate on the Epistles of S. Paul. The only parts which the writer possessed were those on Romans and 1 Corinthians.

(5) An exposition of Alcuin's views on the honour to be shown to Holy Scripture, and on the importance of its teaching for ourselves, is contained in a letter which he wrote to a Continental abbess named Gisla.[4] He urges her to exercise herself in the reading of these Books. " God Himself and our Lord speaks to thee through them." The analogy of an embassy is employed. " Lo ! from heaven, the King of Kings— yea, thy own Spouse—through Prophets, Apostles, and Teachers, hath deigned to send His letters to thee, O maiden. . . . Let the careful reading of these letters refresh thee, because in them God is known, in them the glory of eternal life is revealed, in them is shown what we ought to believe, to hope, to love, to avoid."

(6) Alcuin wishes the Word of God to be read at episcopal banquets. " It is fitting that a reader should be heard there, not a harper ; the sermons of Fathers,

[1] Mon. Mog. p. 213.   [2] V. sup. p. 61.
[3] Mon. Mog. pp. 97-98.   [4] Mon. Alc. pp. 177-180.

not the songs of Gentiles." [1] He tells the Kentish people that *ignorantia scripturarum ignorantia Dei est*.[2] " Get for yourselves," he says, " teachers and masters of the Holy Scripture ; lest there be among you a poverty of the Word of God, or persons be wanting who can rule the people of God ; lest the font of truth be dried up in your midst." He exhorts that the young men at York should be instructed in the wisdom of Holy Scripture, " so that the light of knowledge which from the beginning of the Faith has shone in our Church (*i.e.* York) may never be extinguished, but to the praise and honour of God may grow bright in many places." [3] Exhortations of a similar kind are addressed to the community at Hexham.[4]

(ii) Prayer

Numerous requests are made in these letters for prayer, sometimes on behalf of the writers themselves in their spiritual difficulties, sometimes on behalf of the work in which they were engaged. The following illustrations may suffice :

(*a*) *Bede*. In a letter to Acca, we have a request for the prayers of those who read the writer's exposition of S. Mark's Gospel. " Before all things, I beseech . . . all those who perchance will read this work that they will intercede with the Righteous Judge for my

---

[1] Mon. Alc. p. 357. [2] *Ibid.* p. 370.
[3] *Ibid.* p. 255. [4] *Ibid.* p. 375.

DOCTRINE AND DEVOTION 75

frailties both of body and mind." [1] Similarly, in the
letter to Albinus which is prefixed to the *Ecclesiastical
History*, there is a request for prayer. "I humbly
beseech thee, most loved father, that you will
remember, together with the servants of Christ who
are with you, carefully to intercede for my frailty with
the Righteous Judge ; and that you will admonish
those, to whom you cause these same works of ours to
come, to do this same thing."

(b) *Boniface*. In a letter to the abbess Eadburga,
which is permeated by the spirit of prayer, Boniface
asks prayers both for himself and for pagans. [2] The
letter was evidently written in a time of deep de-
spondency. "Everywhere is labour, everywhere is
grief. There are fightings without, there are fears
within." He alludes to the snares laid by "false
brethren." [3] So he begs Eadburga to pray for him.
She was to ask "the Righteous Defender of our life,
and the One salutary refuge of those who are in trouble,
the Lamb of God, Who has taken away the sins of the
world," to keep him unharmed by means of a protecting Right Hand. She was to ask "that the most

[1] Migne, *P.L.* xciv. 689.
[2] Mon. Mog. pp. 211-212.
[3] More explicitly, he tells us elsewhere (*ibid.* p. 158) that while *he*
was striving to sow the good seed of the Word, there were "false priests
and hypocrites" who would sow tares upon it, striving to choke it or to
mar its growth. "What we plant, these men do not water, so that it
may grow, but they strive to root it up, so that it may wither." They
were deceivers of the people, "offering and teaching new sects and
errors of diverse kind." On opposition offered by "false brethren" in
Thuringia, see *Vita Bonf.* c. 6.

Righteous Father would enable him to gird up his loins, would place burning torches in his hands, and would enlighten the hearts of the Gentiles so that they might behold the Gospel of the glory of Christ." He concludes his letter with a request that Eadburga would pray " for those pagans who have been committed to us by the Apostolic See : that the Saviour of the world would snatch them from the worship of idols and join them to the sons of the one mother, the Catholic Church, to the praise and glory of His Name, Who willeth all men to be saved and to come to the knowledge of the truth."

About the time when Bede completed his *Ecclesiastical History*, a bishop (Pecthelm) had been appointed to the newly-constituted see of Whithern (Candida Casa).[1] This place—so familiar because of its associations with Ninian—was now part of Northumbrian territory. We should like to know more about Pecthelm and his work in this Northern outpost. At one time he had been associated with Aldhelm.[2] Boniface was somewhat perplexed because it was asserted in many quarters that it was not lawful for a man to marry a widow for whose son he had previously been a sponsor at Baptism. He consults Pecthelm on this question, and at the same time he asks the help of that bishop's prayers.[3] The bishop is asked to pray that Boniface, " while striving to offer the light of Gospel truth to persons who are blind, who do not

[1] H.E. v. 23.   [2] *Ibid.* v. 18.   [3] Mon. Mog. pp. 94-95.

know their own darkness and are unwilling to see, may not be involved in the darkness of his own sins, and may not run or have run in vain ; but, strengthened by intercessions, may press on, stainless and enlightened, to the light of eternity."

A remarkable letter is one in which Boniface asks *all* English Christians to pray for the conversion of pagan Saxons.[1] It was a prayer for their own kinsfolk, who deserved compassion, inasmuch as (so these pagan Saxons were in the habit of saying) they were " of one blood and of one bone." Christians at home were to pray that " the Word of the Lord might have free course and be glorified . . . that God and our Lord Jesus Christ . . . would convert to the Catholic Faith the hearts of the pagan Saxons ; that they might recover from the snares of the devil, by which they were held captive, and might be joined to the sons of Mother Church."

Boniface had a real love of country, and it must have been a great comfort to him to feel that he and his companions were not fighting single-handed against the forces of paganism, but that, by means of mutual prayer, many of his countrymen and countrywomen were sharing in the struggle. It may be noted that he was assured of the prayers of his own archbishop (Brihtwald) at the very outset of his missionary career.[2]

(c) *Lullus.* Friends at home assure Lullus of their

[1] Mon. Mog. pp. 107-108 ; H. & S. iii. 313.   [2] Mon. Mog. p. 96.

prayers. Cyneheard, bishop of Winchester, says in one of his letters : " We are mindful of you always in our prayers." [1] Guthbert, abbot of Wearmouth and Jarrow, remembers him in daily prayer. [2] Cynewulf, king of the West-Saxons, writes to him and speaks of mutual prayer. [3]

(d) *Alcuin*. In a letter addressed to Ethelbert, bishop of Hexham, and to " the whole congregation of those who serve God in the church of S. Andrew," Alcuin commends himself to the prayers of that community. [4] He begs their prayers both at the Canonical Hours and at their private devotions ; so that, by means of these prayers, he may be " loosed from the chains of his sins," and with the beloved brethren of Hexham " may merit an entrance through the gates of life."

In a specially solemn passage in one of his letters to Eanbald II., he speaks of the possibility of his own approaching decease. [5] He was " weighed down with old age and infirmity," and thought of the Day of Judgment. " Do thou, most faithful son, labour for the soul of thy father, whether he is now remaining in this frame of dust, or then hastening to judgment ; that it may have rest, and pardon of its sins ; that the stains which have clung to it from its defiled habitation in the body may be washed away by a brother's intercession."

[1] Mon. Mog. p. 287.   [2] *Ibid.* p. 290.   [3] *Ibid.* pp. 306–307.
[4] Mon. Alc. p. 374   [5] *Ibid.* p. 336.

Instances are recorded of prayers for the departed.[1]
A friendship had been formed *in occiduis regionibus*
between Boniface and a man named Dynne, whose
daughter Lioba writes, eight years after her father's
death, and asks the prayers of Boniface for her father's
soul.[2] Ethelbert II., king of Kent, asks the prayers of
this same missionary for himself, both in his lifetime,
and in the event of his own pre-decease.[3] The names
of persons sent by Lullus were directed by Cyneheard,
bishop of Winchester, throughout the monasteries and
churches of his diocese, so that masses might be celebrated for them and prayers said.[4] Lullus was asked
to do the same with regard to a list to be sent to him by
the bishop.[5] It seems to have been much a similar
arrangement to that which is proposed in a letter
addressed to Boniface by Elfwald, king of the East-
Angles.[6] " The names of the departed, and of those
who were entering on the way of all flesh, would be
brought forth on either side." So in a letter addressed
to Lullus by Alhred, king of Northumbria, and queen
Osgeofu.[7] The names of persons contained in a list
sent by the missionary were daily presented in prayer
before God in all the monasteries within the royal
jurisdiction. The same missionary commends to

[1] We hear from other sources of this practice. In the church at
Ripon, Wilfrid's name was remembered daily in prayer (Eddius, c. 17).
[2] Mon. Mog. p. 83. Lioba afterwards became abbess of Bischoffsheim.
[3] *Ibid.* pp. 255-256.   [4] *Ibid.* p. 270.   [5] *Ibid.* l.c.
[6] *Ibid.* pp. 210-211 ; H. & S. iii. 387-388.
[7] *Ibid.* pp. 284-285 ; iii. 434.

Albert, archbishop of York, the names of brothers and friends departing from the light of this life.[1]   A similar commendation is made in a letter to Guthbert.[2]

Alcuin says that " the prayers of the living help the dying, both for the forgiveness of their sins and for the increase of greater glory." [3]   Writing to the bishops of his own land, he tells them that King Charles much desires their prayers " for himself, for the stability of his kingdom, for the extension of the Christian Name, and for the soul of the most blessed father, Pope Adrian." [4]   He himself consoles that king on the death of Queen Liudgarda,[5] and definitely prays for her : " Lord God Jesus, mild and merciful, have pity on her whom Thou hast taken from us," and so on.[6]

Cuthbert, we are told, could never celebrate Mass without giving way to tears.[7]   Alcuin did not possess the " gift of tears."   When he prayed, he would do so with hands outstretched, and with many groans.[8]

(iii) THE SACRAMENTS

(a) Baptism.   Bede was eager to get something like a settled ministry in out-of-the-way parts of

---

[1] Mon. Mog. p. 288.   [2] Ibid. p. 289.

[3] Mon. Alc. p. 375.

[4] Ibid. p. 296.   For the estimation in which King Charles held that pontiff's memory, see S.D. p. 33.   He asks King Offa to give orders that intercessions should be made for Adrian's soul (Mon. Alc. p. 289).

[5] On Liudgarda and the monastery of Fladbury, see Mon. Alc. p. 294.

[6] Ibid. pp. 534–535.   [7] Vita Cutb. c. 16.   [8] Vita Alch. c. 8.

Northumbria.[1] He urges Egbert to get more helpers, with a view to meet the religious needs of some of the people under his care. Especially were these additional helpers needed for the administration of Baptism.[2]

Like Bede, Boniface had a high conception of this Sacrament. He and other bishops state : " Our Father without doubt is God Who created us, our Mother is the Church which spiritually regenerated us in Baptism." [3] But it would seem that Boniface needed some fuller instruction. Pope Gregory II. reminds him of the ancient custom of the Church, viz. that " whoever has been baptised in the Name of the Father, the Son, and the Holy Ghost, it is by no means lawful that he should be re-baptised." [4] This all-important point—was Baptism administered in the Name of the Holy Trinity, or was it not ?—is elaborated by Pope Zacharias.[5]

(b) *Holy Communion.* It was customary to ask for the celebration of Masses on behalf of the deceased.[6] Bugge prefers such a request in a letter to Boniface.[7] " I beg that you will offer the oblations of sacred Masses for the soul of my kinsman, who was dear to me before all others, whose name was N." Guthbert had received a list of names from Lullus, and tells him that

---

[1] *Ep. ad Egb.* §§ 5, 7. [2] *Ibid.* § 5. [3] Mon. Mog. p. 174.
[4] *Ibid.* p. 90. Cf. *ibid.* pp. 167-168 ; H. & S. iii. 406 (*Dialogue* of Egbert).
[5] Mon. Mog. p. 186.
[6] Cf. Eddius, c. 65, where we are told that it was decided to celebrate a private Mass for Wilfrid every day.
[7] Mon. Mog. pp. 74-76.

these names had been added to those of members of the monastery who were asleep in Christ, so that he had ordered ninety and more Masses to be celebrated for them.[1]

It may be noted that Bede seems to have entertained grave doubt as to the efficacy of such Masses in the case of persons who, in their lifetime, paid but little regard to the claims of religion.[2]

An English abbot named Sigebald tells Boniface that his name is included with the names of the abbot's own bishops at the celebration of Mass.[3] The same missionary is assured by Torthelm, bishop of Leicester, that he is remembered " in the sacred celebrations of Masses and in daily prayers." [4]

There is a famous passage in which Bede is speaking of " daily reception of the Body and Blood of the Lord," and of the infrequency with which the laity communicated.[5] Even the more devout among them only did so at Christmas, Epiphany, and Easter, although there were innumerable people of both sexes and of varied ages who might well have done so " every Lord's Day, and on the Feasts of the Holy Apostles and Martyrs."

Alcuin wrote a letter to Edilburga (daughter of Offa), who was abbess of Fladbury.[6] He sent her a

---

[1] Mon. Mog. p. 290. [2] Ep. ad Egb. § 17.
[3] Mon. Mog. p. 167. [4] Ibid. p. 252.
[5] Ep. ad Egb. § 15. Cf. exhortation to frequent Communion which is given in twenty-third canon, Council of Clovesho. H. & S. iii. 370.
[6] Mon. Alc. pp. 293-294. Edilburga is mentioned in one of Offa's monastic charters (K.C.D. cli.).

paten and a chalice, and strongly advocated a daily
oblation to God. " Apostolic authority," he says,
" has appointed this custom, therefore it is not to be
omitted, but diligently followed." It was his own
practice, as we read elsewhere, to celebrate Mass
daily.[1] It may be noted that Pope Gregory II., in
writing to Boniface, favours the use of *one* chalice only.
" It is not fitting," he says, " to place two or three
chalices on the altar when Mass is celebrated." [2]

Several illustrations may be found in these letters
of a belief which coloured our devotional life, viz. the
protecting influence of saints.[3]

(1) Cuthbert, archbishop of Canterbury, writes a
letter of consolation to Lullus after Boniface's death·
He speaks of the martyred missionary as one who would
be a patron for them, together with Gregory and
Augustine, in the presence of Christ.[4] The prayers of
Apostles, Martyrs, etc., were to be asked, so that the
Grace of Christ would enable the survivors to persevere
in their appointed work.[5] In proportion as Boniface
was now in closer fellowship than before with Almighty
God, so his influence with Him would be greater.[6]

(2) Milred, bishop of Worcester, emphasises the

[1] *Vita Alch.* c. 13. Cf. H.A.A. § 33.

[2] Mon. Mog. p. 89. On horn patens and chalices, *v. sup.* p. 29.

[3] In the vision at Meaux, Wilfrid was told that years were added
to his life. This result was partly due to the intercession of the Blessed
Virgin (Eddius, c. 56). The belief was expressed, after Wilfrid's own
death, that for his friends he was " in the sight of God, a guardian and
defender without ceasing " (*ibid.* c. 68).

[4] Mon. Mog. p. 263.   [5] *Ibid.* p. 265.   [6] *Ibid.* l.c.

same thought. He had heard the sad news of Boniface's death. But he might not lawfully speak of it as sad, seeing that we had sent such a patron to the Heavenly Kingdom, and that we believed we should, by God's help, be supported by his holy intercessions.[1]

(3) The monastery at Jarrow had been founded in honour of S. Paul.[2] As we have already seen, Guthbert believed he had lived under the protection of that Apostle for forty-six years.[3]

(4) Alcuin writes to bishop Higbald and the monks of Lindisfarne. His thoughts are of the recent calamity when the Northmen had ravaged the holy places. He exhorts the members who were left. " Call back to you," he says, " your patrons, who have forsaken you for a time. Power was not wanting to them with a merciful God. But, we know not why, they kept silence."[4]

Just as there was a belief in the protecting influence of saints, so there was a belief in the malignant influence of demons. In order to guard against these attacks, Bede advises that people should be taught to sign themselves with the Sign of the Cross.[5] The anonymous biographer of Alcuin opens his narrative with a curious story. We read of a visitation of evil spirits.

---

[1] Mon. Mog. p. 267.   [2] H.A.B. § 7.
[3] V. sup. p. 67. We have also seen (v. sup. p. 65) how Hwaetbert held a conviction that Ceolfrid would be an intercessor and protector in Heaven. Cf. H.E. v. 22, on the patrocinium of Egbert, the missionary to Iona.
[4] Mon. Alc. p. 191.   [5] Ep. ad Ego. § 15. Cf. H.E. v. 21.

Alcuin fortifies himself with the Sign of the Cross, chants a Psalm, and the evil spirits disappear.[1] Eagerness shown in the acquisition of relics, and the veneration attached to them, are familiar features of early English religious life. Benedict Biscop brought relics from Rome.[2] Wilfrid was in Rome on three different occasions. We are told that on each occasion when he left that city he took " holy relics " with him.[3] Acca, we are told, brought relics from all parts —he had been with Wilfrid abroad—and placed them in the church at Hexham, dedicating altars to the various saints.[4] A woman named Egburg, who had passed through much sorrow, begs Boniface to send her the consolation either of holy relics or of a letter written by himself.[5] Alcuin, in a letter to Angilbertus (an official of King Pippin), shows special eagerness to obtain " gifts most sweet and much necessary to himself, i.e. the relics of saints." [6]

[1] *Vita Alch.* c. 1. Cf. *ibid.* c. 12 *ad fin.*, for the way in which Alcuin repelled the approach of the Devil. In the story (H.E. v. 2) about the healing of the dumb boy, we read that the bishop (John of Hexham), after telling the boy to put out his tongue, made the Sign of the Cross on it.

[2] H.A.B. § 6.

[3] Eddius, cc. 5, 33, 55. This writer was horrified (c. 34) because Queen Eormenburg took away Wilfrid's reliquary and wore it as an ornament. She wore it both in her chamber and when riding in her chariot.

[4] H.E. v. 20.

[5] Mon. Mog. p. 66.

[6] Mon. Alc. pp. 149–150. For the use of relics in procession on the Rogation Days, see 16th canon, Council of Clovesho. H. & S. iii. 368. When Wilfrid's body was brought to its resting place at Ripon, all the monks came out " with holy relics " to meet the *cortège*. Eddius, c. 66.

CHAPTER VI

LEARNING

THIS subject has already been touched upon in the chapters on the Episcopate and on Monastic Life. But fuller treatment is desirable. We shall seek to gather up, from contemporary letters, a few particulars regarding the learning of Aldhelm, Bede, Boniface, Lullus, and Alcuin ; to show the fame which some of these persons enjoyed as teachers, and the reputation in which their works were held.[1]

(i) ALDHELM

This famous abbot of Malmesbury, whose learning is so highly eulogised by Bede, became bishop of Sherborne when the West-Saxon diocese was divided in A.D. 705.[2] His episcopate was a short one, as he died in A.D. 709.

Probably no man in those days enjoyed a greater reputation for learning. A Scot, " of unknown name,"

---

[1] Comparatively little will be said about Aldhelm, whose activities belong more to the previous century.

[2] H.E. v. 18. For another eulogy of Aldhelm's learning, see G.R. i. 31. Cf. G.P., Book v.

writes and asks him to be his teacher.[1] This Scot
would rather learn from Aldhelm, who was "a very
pure well of knowledge," than drink from the muddy
well of any other teacher. He concludes his letter
with a request for the loan of a book, which he will not
keep longer than two weeks.

Aldhelm himself, in the days before the division of
the diocese, writes to Haeddi, bishop of the West-
Saxons.[2] He had hoped to visit that prelate after
Christmas, but was prevented. The special value of
the letter lies in the account which the writer gives of
his own studies and of their nature. These studies
certainly seem to have been of an involved and an
abstruse kind—technical points with regard to the
metrical art, astrological calculations as to the signs of
the zodiac, and such-like.[3]

Of far more real interest than the letter to bishop
Haeddi is a letter which Aldhelm wrote (A.D. 705) at
the command of a West-Saxon synod.[4] It was
addressed to Geruntius (Geraint), king of Damnonia
(Devon and Cornwall), and to all the priests in that
kingdom. It was on the subject of "the unity of the
Catholic Church and concord in the Christian
religion." He deplores "the grave schism and cruel
scandal" which had arisen in the Church of Christ.

[1] Mon. Mog. p. 34.   [2] *Ibid.* pp. 32-34.
[3] Aldhelm's learning is undoubted, but his style is turgid, and the
subjects on which he wrote have largely ceased to possess the interest
which they once aroused.
[4] Mon. Mog. pp. 24-31 ; H. & S. iii. 268-273.

Then he goes on to treat of the tonsure and of the Paschal questions. The British tonsure, he believes, can be traced in its origin to Simon Magus, the Roman tonsure to S. Peter. Having spoken of the Paschal question,[1] he passes on to what is the most interesting part of his letter—the description of the un-Christian conduct of British priests across the Severn.[2] Then he makes his final appeal on behalf of the teaching of S. Peter and the tradition of the Roman Church. " The Catholic Faith," he says, " and the concord of brotherly charity go inseparably together in the same path." It is in vain for any one to boast of the Catholic Faith, " if he does not follow the teaching and the rule of S. Peter."

We can recognise the ability of this letter, even if we do not always agree with the views expressed. The arguments used were exactly of the kind best calculated to impress the readers, and these arguments are backed by specious quotations from Holy Scripture. It is not surprising to read that the letter succeeded—partially, at least—in effecting its object. We are told that " many of the Britons who were subject to the West Saxons were led to the Catholic celebration of the Lord's Passover." [3]

[1] Cf. H.E. v. 21—Ceolfrid's letter to Naiton (Nechtan), king of the Picts—for treatment of both questions.

[2] This description reveals an acme of bitterness and contempt on the part of the British Christians towards their Saxon neighbours. The British attitude was intelligible, though not defensible. For a parallel instance of uncharitableness (though in quite another connection), see Eddius, c. 49.

[3] H.E. v. 18.

The posthumous fame of Aldhelm may be illustrated from a letter written by Lullus to his old teacher, Dealwin. He there requests that some of Aldhelm's works, prose or verse, should be sent " for the consolation of my pilgrimage, and in memory of the blessed bishop himself." [1]

(ii) BEDE

In the short autobiographical notice inserted in the concluding chapter of the *Ecclesiastical History*, Bede tells us that he always found delight in learning, teaching, and writing.[2] This statement is fully borne out by various passages in the letters we are considering. Perhaps the most interesting testimony of all is that of his old pupil, Guthbert, which has already been quoted.[3]

Bede's facilities for study had been greatly increased by the literary zeal of Benedict Biscop and of Ceolfrid. The former collected books both at Rome and elsewhere.[4] He gave instructions as to the care to be taken of these books.[5] The latter had added to their number.[6] As Symeon of Durham well says : " Bede had before his eyes an abundance of books of every kind, which his own abbot Benedict . . . had brought into the monastery." [7]

[1] Mon. Mog. p. 215.
[2] William of Malmesbury (G.R. i. 66) has the following lament over the death of Bede : " sepulta est cum eo gestorum omnis pene notitia usque ad nostra tempora."
[3] *V. sup.* p. 66.   [4] H.A.B. §§ 4, 6, 9.   [5] *Ibid.* § 11.
[6] *Ibid.* § 15 ; H.A.A. § 20.   [7] S.D. p. 136.

The reputation in which Bede's works were held was very great. Boniface on more than one occasion asks for copies to be sent to him.[1] Sometimes the request was in general terms, but we also find particular works specified (the *Homilies*, the commentary on the Proverbs of Solomon).[2] We have already noticed works for which Lullus asked in a letter to Albert, archbishop of York.[3] He also writes to Guthbert, asking for Bede's works on the building of the Temple and on the Song of Songs—both of them, if possible, but especially the former.[4] It is satisfactory to know that Guthbert was able to send it to him.[5] It was this same abbot who sent him the *Lives of Cuthbert* (prose and verse).[6]

Special mention may be made of a letter which Bede wrote to Nothelm, a London presbyter who became archbishop of Canterbury.[7] From this letter it is clear that a literary fellowship existed between the two men. It is this same Nothelm who is mentioned in the letter to Albinus which we find prefixed to the *Ecclesiastical History*, and whose literary help is gratefully acknowledged in the Preface to that work.

(iii) BONIFACE

Willibald waxes eloquent in his biography when he speaks of Boniface as a pupil and as a teacher during

---

[1] Mon. Mog. pp. 180, 181, 250. [2] *Ibid.* p. 250.
[3] *V. sup.* pp. 51–52. [4] Mon. Mog. p. 289. [5] *Ibid.* p. 290.
[6] *V. sup.* p. 61. [7] Migne, *P.L.* xciv. 687.

the earlier days in England.[1] Our letters give additional confirmation. Pope Gregory II., when authorising the mission to pagans, speaks of Boniface as one who " from infancy had learned sacred letters." [2] Of even more importance is the testimony of his own bishop, Daniel. Boniface was " signally adorned with manifold knowledge and with the grace of various virtues." [3] He had been " excellently educated in Divine volumes." [4] We also have the testimony of his pupils. An unnamed pupil sends verses composed by himself to two women, who had befriended him in time of illness, and says that it was from Boniface that he had learned the metrical art.[5] Another pupil addresses him in terms of the deepest affection and respect, speaking of him as " a most devoted teacher in the study of letters." [6]

We know how gratefully he received books sent to him by friends in England, and how frequently he asks for books. Bugge is requested to send him the *passiones martyrum*, and she wishes him to send her some " collections " of Holy Scripture (presumably made by himself).[7] Daniel is requested to send him abbot Winbert's book on the Prophets.[8] Egbert and Hwaetbert are requested to send works of Bede.[9] Other requests of a similar nature are made by him. It is clear that, even in his busy days as a missionary, he

[1] *Vita Bonf.* c. 2. [2] Mon. Mog. p. 62. [3] *Ibid.* p. 161.
[4] *Ibid.* p. 162. [5] *Ibid.* p. 243. [6] *Ibid.* p. 247.
[7] *Ibid.* p. 75. [8] *V. sup.* p. 61.
[9] Mon. Mog. pp. 180, 181, 250.

had not ceased to be a learner.[1] He had realised the truth of the Scriptural saying that, if he was to teach others, he must teach himself. His life well illustrates the spirit of Alcuin's dictum, *qui non discit, non docet*.[2]

(iv) LULLUS

Like his predecessor, Lullus was a lover of learning. He asks his friends in England to send him books—works of Aldhelm, works of Bede.[3] His own literary help was once asked by his kinsman Cyneheard, bishop of Winchester.[4] The bishop was anxious to get any spiritual consolations to be found in ancient books not possessed by himself. He was also anxious to see books on secular knowledge—*e.g.* on medicine—which he did not know, and which Lullus might happen to acquire.

(v) ALCUIN [5]

Alcuin speaks of " the light of knowledge which from the beginning of the Faith had shone in the church of York." [6] Of that church he calls himself a son.[7] In it, he tells us, he had been brought up and

---

[1] Cf. *Vita Bonf.* c. 3, on Boniface's studies of Holy Scripture.
[2] Mon. Alc. p. 375.
[3] Mon. Mog. pp. 215, 288, 289.
[4] *Ibid.* pp. 269–270.
[5] A notable eulogy is pronounced upon Alcuin by William of Malmesbury, who speaks of him (G.R. i. 68–69) as the most learned English writer, next to Aldhelm and Bede, that he has read.
[6] Mon. Alc. p. 255.   [7] *Ibid.* pp. 252, 295.

educated.[1] He writes a letter, full of affection, to the
" most beloved and exceedingly venerable brethren in
the love of Christ " who belong to that church, and he
gratefully acknowledges his own debt to them.[2] They
had cherished his tender years, they had watched
over him in the critical days of adolescence, they had
strengthened him with discipline and learning.
He had been fortunate in having Egbert and Albert
as his teachers. He had also been fortunate in the
fact that the York school possessed a noble library,
some of the contents of which he describes in his well-
known poem.[3] It would seem that he himself had
been made heir by his " beloved master " (*i.e.* Albert)
to some of the treasures in that library.[4] Some of
these books had been gathered through the industry
of his master, some by himself.[5] At a later stage in his
career on the Continent, he felt the need of some of
these books for the educational work he was carrying
on in the monastery of S. Martin at Tours, and he
wished the help of King Charles in having books sent
over to him.[6]

Alcuin wrote many works.[7] A list is given in the
ninth century anonymous *Life*.[8] The works were
certainly of a varied and a comprehensive kind. They
include treatises on the Holy Trinity and on the nature

[1] Mon. Alc. p. 331.   [2] *Ibid.* p. 249.
[3] *De Pontif. Ebor.* 1535 ff.   [4] Mon. Alc. p. 331.
[5] *Ibid* p. 346.   [6] *Ibid.* pp. 345–346.
[7] *Vita Alch.* c. 12—" scribens multa omni ecclesiae utilia."
[8] *Ibid.* l.c.

of the soul. There were treatises on Genesis and on the Psalms. There were commentaries on S. John's Gospel and on various Pauline Epistles. Homilies on the principal virtues and vices appeared, also Homilies taken from the works of the Fathers. Grammar, rhetoric, dialectic, orthography, and music were also dealt with.

We think of him mainly as a teacher. In touching terms, he exhorts the younger brethren of York not to forget their old master in their prayers.[1] He had always desired their progress in ecclesiastical discipline and in spiritual teaching. Whether he was present or absent, he would always be their well-wisher. His zeal as a teacher is even more strikingly shown in a letter which he wrote to King Charles.[2] He there describes the educational work at Tours. He will do his best " to sow the seeds of wisdom " among the monks. " In the morning, when studies flourished in the heyday of youth, I sowed in Britain ; but now, when blood is growing cold, as it were at evening, I cease not to sow in Francia."

Interest in individual pupils is shown. This appears in a letter which he wrote to Offa, king of Mercia.[3] The pupil sent to that king had been a good learner, and the king was to see that his time was well occupied. A wish is expressed for the pupil's good success. " The success of my pupils is my reward with God."

Willingness to teach is expressed in a letter written

[1] Mon. Alc. p. 250.　　[2] *Ibid.* pp. 344-348.　　[3] *Ibid.* p. 265.

by Alcuin to Higbald, bishop of Lindisfarne.[1] Their common son, Candidus, had stayed for a considerable time with Alcuin on the Continent, had been instructed by him, and then sent back. If he came again, he would receive further instruction. " Whatever things I have learned from masters which tend to help the holy Churches of God, these things I am delighted to communicate, especially to the people of our nation ; and not to them only, but to all who earnestly seek them ; if I can do anything useful for spiritual progress and for the increase of the holy Church of God."

Exhortations to study abound. Ethelheard, archbishop of Canterbury, is exhorted to see to it that in the house of God are found young men who read, a choir of singers, and the use of books. In this way the dignity of Canterbury might be revived.[2] In a letter to bishop Ethelbert and the community at Hexham, the necessity of " the reading of sacred books " is emphasised.[3] The great traditions of Hexham were seemingly in the writer's mind when he pointed out the impossibility, or the virtual impossibility, of such a place being safe without teachers.[4]

Not only does Alcuin exhort to study, but he advocates *method* in study. In a letter to Eanbald II., he speaks about orderly arrangements for the work of teaching.[5] These were designed to prevent idleness

[1] Mon. Alc. pp. 146–147.   [2] *Ibid.* p. 367.   [3] *Ibid.* p. 375.
[4] On the great traditions, see Raine, *Hexham*, i. xiv. ff.
[5] Mon. Alc. p. 335.

on the part of the pupils, " lest, with no occupation, they wander about in different places, or engage in useless games, or give themselves up to other follies."

The literary interests of the above five men—Aldhelm, Bede, Boniface, Lullus, Alcuin—constitute a bright feature in the history of a somewhat depressing century. Another illustrious quintette may be found in Acca, Albinus, Daniel, Egbert, Albert. Of all of them we have already had occasion to speak, but Acca calls for fuller mention. Bede pronounces a notable eulogy upon him.[1] *Inter alia*, we are told that he was " most learned in sacred letters." He was a sedulous collector of books, and formed a " most ample and most noble library " at Hexham. This included the stories of the passions of the martyrs. There were also other " ecclesiastical volumes," the nature of which not specified.[2]

He had been the devoted friend and confidant of Wilfrid, whom he accompanied when the latter set out for Rome in order to prosecute his second appeal. He was with him when a visit was paid to Willibrord in Frisia.[3] He was the recipient of his master's confidence regarding the visions seen in Sussex [4] and at Meaux.[5] On his master's death, he succeeded to the see of Hexham. Eventually, for some

---

[1] H.E. v. 20. Cf. Aelred of Rievaux's eulogy (*De Sanctis Hagust.*, c. 6).
[2] On this library, cf. Raine, *u.s.* i. 31–32, note g.
[3] H.E. iii. 13.   Hence a tale (*ibid.* l.c.) related by the missionary.
[4] Eadmer, *Vita Wilf.* c. 43.
[5] Eddius, c. 56.

reason that is not clear, he was driven from that see.[1]
But he was buried at Hexham, and two stone crosses
were placed, one at his head, and one at his feet.[2]

A debt of gratitude is due to him for literary
encouragement which he gave. It was due to his
instigation (together with that of Tatberht, abbot of
Ripon) that Eddius wrote the well-known biography,
Vita Wilfridi Episcopi.[3] An interesting letter from Acca
to Bede has come down to us.[4] Acca had often sug-
gested to his friend, both in conversation and by
letter, that, after his commentary on the Acts of the
Apostles, he should write one on S. Luke's Gospel.
But Bede was reluctant to do so. One reason was the
difficulty of the task, another was the fact that
S. Ambrose had already written a commentary on that
Gospel. Acca, however, still adhered to his purpose.
He urged his friend to undertake the task, jocosely telling
him to expound the blessed Luke " luculento sermone."

Earlier in the chapter, brief mention has been made
of Nothelm. He had rendered valuable help to Bede,
it being recorded of him that he had " thoroughly
searched the archives of the holy Roman Church,"
finding some epistles of Gregory and other pontiffs.[5]
His help is once asked by Boniface.[6] The latter wished

---

[1] S.D. p. 11. Prior Richard cannot throw any light on the cause of
the expulsion. " Qua autem urgente necessitate pulsus sit vel quo
diverterit, scriptum non repperi " (*Hist. Hagust.* i. 15).

[2] S.D. p. 14.   [3] See Preface to that work.

[4] Raine, *u.s.* i. 33-34.   [5] H.E. Pref.

[6] Mon. Mog. pp. 95-97 ; H. & S. iii. 335-336.

to obtain a copy of the epistle which was said to contain Augustine's questions and Gregory's answers. Nothelm is asked to find out if the above epistle really was written by Gregory or not. The archivists of the Roman Church could not find it among the other epistles of that pontiff. Nothelm is also asked to tell Boniface " in what year from the Incarnation of Christ did the first preachers, sent by S. Gregory, come to the English people."

Bede speaks of the glorious days when Theodore and Hadrian were teaching in England.[1] These days could not be recalled. In his own days, there was too much of what he terms—in his letter to Hwaetbert—the inertia of the English people, and their luke-warmness in study.[2] We have already seen, however, that he pays generous tributes to the learning of several of his contemporaries.[3] The greater part of his own life was covered by the long archiepiscopate at Canterbury of Brihtwald, followed by the short one of Tatwin. Of the learning of both of these men he speaks favourably. It is true, the praise in the former case is qualified by the remark that Brihtwald was not to be compared with his predecessor, Theodore.[4] In the latter case, the praise is very warm. Tatwin, he says, was " nobly instructed in sacred letters." [5]

It is clear that the love of learning was by no means dead.

---

[1] H.E. iv. 2.   [2] Migne, P.L. xciv. 697.
[3] V. sup. pp. 41, 69, 96.   [4] H.E. v. 8.   [5] Ibid. v. 23.

CHAPTER VII

SOCIAL LIFE

FROM these letters we get glimpses at times of how people ate and drank, of how they dressed, and of the sports in which they indulged.

(i) EATING AND DRINKING

It would seem that immoderation in food and drink was a characteristic of our Anglo-Saxon forefathers. After the dedication of the church at Ripon in Wilfrid's time, we read that a great feast was held, lasting three days and three nights.[1] Possibly, however, the idea was to allow the people of Ripon and neighbourhood to participate in the rejoicings. Hence we can understand why the feast was of such a protracted character. Wilfrid, we read, was not " given to wine." [2]

Bede speaks of the report that some bishops had among their companions persons who were addicted to gluttony and drunkenness.[3] Boniface speaks of the report that some bishops were themselves addicted to

---

[1] Eddius, c. 17.　　[2] *Ibid.* c. 9.　　[3] *Ep. ad Egb.* § 4.

the latter vice.[1] Alcuin delivers repeated warnings against it. He speaks of " the iniquity of drunkenness, which is the pit of perdition, and much hurtful to servants of God." [2] The monks of Lindisfarne are told " not to destroy in drunkenness the words of their prayers." [3] Bishop Higbald is told to let his feasts be "not in drunkenness, but in sobriety." [4] The brethren of York are told " to flee from drunkenness, as they would flee from the pits of hell." [5] A warning is given to monks against *conviviorum frequentia*, and an abbot is enjoined to see that moderation is practised in food and drink.[6] " Hidden feastings and secret drinking bouts " on the part of monks are condemned. At such banquets demons were present.[7]

The warnings are so frequent that we must believe that Alcuin had definite instances of the evil before him.[8] It may be objected that he was not on the spot, and may have given credence to exaggerated rumours. But we must remember that a considerable part of his life was spent in England, and that he doubtless then had opportunities of judging for himself. Even after his Continental life had begun, he was back in his native land for three years (A.D. 790–793).

[1] *V. sup.* p. 40. He himself, according to his biographer, abstained from wine and strong drink (*Vita Bonf.* c. 3). It was not so with Alcuin, who, we are told, followed the Apostolic counsel contained in 1 Tim. v. 23 (*Vita Alch.* c. 13).
[2] Mon. Alc. p. 194.   [3] *Ibid.* p. 191.   [4] *Ibid.* p. 192.
[5] *Ibid.* p. 251.   [6] *Ibid.* pp. 841, 846.   [7] *Ibid.* p. 200.
[8] His words are very much an echo or an expansion of what we find in the 21st canon, Council of Clovesho. H. & S. iii. 369.

(ii) Dress

It may seem, at first sight, that this is not a subject of first-rate importance, and that the earnestness of denunciation directed against vanity in dress is somewhat overdone. This, however, was not the view taken by responsible persons in that age. To their minds, the evil was of a most serious nature, involving the most disastrous consequences. The whole question of monastic discipline was at stake. The love of vanity in dress tended to the loosening of the bonds of discipline both among monks and clergy, it tended to secularisation of life and to the overthrow of religious ideals. It was a widespreading canker which must be cast out.

That the above is not an exaggerated estimate of the situation may be seen if we examine, first of all, the authoritative teaching of the English Church as set forth in the Council of Clovesho,[1] and afterwards if we examine some of the letters in which the subject is treated. The 19th canon of the above Council tells monks and nuns not to wear " showy garments which —after the manner of secular folk—minister to vain glory, but to be clothed in a simple habit befitting their profession." The 20th canon tells nuns to devote attention to study and psalmody, rather than to the weaving and embroidering of parti-coloured garments. The 28th canon tells nuns, once they have received the

[1] H. & S. iii. 363 ff.

habit of their profession, not again to have their secular garments, going about "in ornamental and bright clothing, such as in lay life girls are wont to wear."

Boniface is very emphatic on the subject of vanity in dress.[1] Writing to Cuthbert, archbishop of Canterbury, he describes the abuse as being hateful to God. These ornamental garments are a disgrace, they owe their origin to Antichrist, and signify his approach. It is he who by this means cunningly seeks to corrupt monastic life, causing "base meetings, weariness of study and prayer, and the loss of souls." Such coverings "signify poverty of soul, and show signs in themselves of arrogance, pride, wantonness, and vanity."

Alcuin's warnings on the subject become almost wearisome in their iteration. In a letter addressed by him to Ethelred, king of Northumbria, and his nobles, there is a striking passage which is valuable as illustrating the social conditions of the times.[2] He is speaking of immoderation in dress, "beyond the necessity of human nature, beyond the custom of our ancestors," and he points the contrast between rich and poor. "This superfluity of princes is the poverty of the people. . . . Some are burdened with a mass of clothing, others perish with cold ; some, like the rich man who was clothed in purple, have abundance of

---

[1] Mon. Mog. p. 209.
[2] Mon. Alc. pp. 182-183.

delicacies and feasts, and Lazarus before the gate dies of hunger. . . . The satiety of the rich man is the hunger of the poor man."

He warns the monks of Lindisfarne against glorying in vanity of dress. " This is not a glory, but a disgrace, to priests and servants of God." [1] Bishop Higbald is told to let his dress be suitable to his rank, and not himself to be conformed to men of the world in any vanity. [2] It is pointed out that vanity in dress is not seemly in the case of men, and is especially hurtful to monks, " whose praise is to do all things temperately and to live religiously." [3] Writing to an abbot of Wearmouth and Jarrow, he says : " It is a confusion to your life that your fingers should sparkle with gold, and that you should adorn your neck with silken coverings . . . it is better that the soul should be decorated with virtues than that the body should be adorned with coloured robes." [4] Elsewhere, he sums up the whole situation with regard to showiness in dress when he says that " it is vanity and pride, and nothing else, and the destruction of regular (*i.e.* monastic) life." [5]

That the evil which we are considering was widespread may be inferred from what is said about it in the letter written by the legates George and Theophylact to Pope Adrian I. [6] It may also be inferred from what Alcuin says in a letter to Ethelheard,

[1] Mon. Alc. p. 191.   [2] *Ibid.* p. 192.   [3] *Ibid.* p. 193.
[4] *Ibid.* p. 842.   [5] *Ibid.* p. 844.   [6] H. & S. iii. 458.

archbishop of Canterbury.[1] Very emphatically he states in a letter to the Kentish people that " teachers of the truth have perished throughout the churches of Christ. Almost all follow secular vanities." [2]

(iii) SPORTS

The love of sport seems to be innate in our countrymen. We read of horse-racing, fox-hunting, coursing, and falconry in the eighth century. Ecclesiastical authority, however, appears to have looked askance at such sports, so far at least as clergy and monks were concerned. Bede tells a story about John, bishop of Hexham (better known as John of Beverley), and a pupil named Heribald.[3] The bishop was out riding one day on a journey, accompanied by his pupils. They came to a grassy plain, which seemed an ideal place for horse-racing. The young men begged the bishop to allow them to race their horses against one another. Finally, he consented, but only on condition that Heribald took no part in the racing. It proved too much for that pupil to be an inactive spectator (especially as he had an excellent horse). In disregard of the bishop's orders, he joined in the racing, but was thrown from his horse. For a considerable time, he hovered between life and death, but eventually he recovered.[4]

[1] Mon. Alc. p. 368.
[3] H.E. v. 6.
[2] *Ibid.* p. 371.
[4] *V. sup.* p. 41.

The 16th canon of the Council of Clovesho deals with the observance of the Rogation Days.[1] There was evidently much carelessness of observance, as we are told that it was the custom of very many people to indulge in games, horse-racing, and feasting on these Days.

The question of clerical participation in field-sports engaged the attention of Boniface on the Continent. He speaks disapprovingly of Frankish bishops who were *venatores*.[2] He writes to Cuthbert, archbishop of Canterbury, and gives an account of a Council which he had held.[3] One of the decrees of that Council was that servants of God were forbidden hunting, " wandering with dogs in woods," and falconry.[4] This is in harmony with a view expressed by Pope Zacharias. " It is," he says, " a detestable and wicked work that a cleric should be found in games, or should spend his life in hawking or hunting." [5] We have already noticed the advice given by Alcuin to Eanbald II. about not having companions who would run about shouting as they chased foxes.[6] We have also noticed what the same adviser said with regard to the sporting proclivities of the younger members of Wearmouth and Jarrow.[7]

There does not seem to have been ecclesiastical opposition to participation in such sports on the part of

[1] H. & S. iii. 368.   [2] Mon. Mog. p. 113.
[3] *Ibid.* pp. 127 ff., 200 ff.   [4] *Ibid.* p. 202.
[5] *Ibid.* p. 196.   [6] *V. sup.* p. 38.   [7] *V. sup.* p. 63.

laymen. Among the presents sent by Boniface to Ethelbald, king of Mercia, were two falcons.[1] We find Ethelbert II., king of Kent, specially asking Boniface to send him two falcons of a breed which was very rare in Kent.[2]

It would seem that some of the abuses mentioned above grew more pronounced as the century wore on. We may take the case of the monastery at Lindisfarne. Bede expressly says that the old-time simplicity in dress still continued in his day.[3] Possibly the advent of King Ceolwulf as a member of the community marked the beginning of a relaxation of former strictness. We read that " licence was given to the monks of the church of Lindisfarne to drink wine and beer ; for previously they were in the habit of drinking only milk and water, according to the old tradition of S. Aidan." [4]

Social conditions may also be illustrated from references made in these letters to *slavery*. Brihtwald, archbishop of Canterbury, had interested himself in the case of a captive girl, but the request for her freedom which he made to Beorwald, abbot of Glastonbury, proved ineffectual.[5] Troubled by the importunity of her relatives, the archbishop now wrote to Forthere, bishop of Sherborne, the letter being carried by a kinsman of the girl. The bishop was to see that

---

[1] Mon. Mog. p. 213.   [2] *Ibid.* p. 256.   [3] *Vita Cutb.* c. 16.
[4] *Vita Oswaldi*, c. 21, *ap.* S.D. (R.S. ed.).
[5] These two persons both appear in an incident connected with Boniface's earlier life (*Vita Bonf.* c. 4).

the abbot accepted a sum of money to be given to him by this kinsman. Then the girl was to be handed over, and led to a place where " she would be able to spend the remaining part of her life with her own kinsfolk, not in the sadness of slavery, but in the joy of freedom." [1] Another illustration may be found in the case of the two boys, Beiloc and Man, whose freedom had been secured by Lullus and his father. [2]

Any one who reads these letters must be struck by the frequent instances of the pleasant custom according to which presents were sent by friends abroad to friends at home, and *vice versâ*. The presents were of the most varied kind ; and they help us, in some degree, to picture the social and the ecclesiastical conditions of the age. The following list may not be without interest :

From Boniface.

He sends (1) to bishop Pecthelm, an " embroidered corporal," [3] also a towel " for wiping the feet of the servants of God " ; [4] (2) to bishop Daniel, a chasuble, " not all of silk, but mixed with goat's wool," also a

---

[1] Mon. Mog. pp. 48–49 ; H. & S. iii. 284.

[2] Mon. Mog. p. 110. We are told that Aidan was in the habit of ransoming slaves, many of whom he would afterwards train for the priesthood (H.E. iii. 5). Among Wilfrid's good deeds, mention is made of the redemption of captives (Eddius, c. 11). The thirty boys whom Willibrord took away with him after his visit to the Danes were probably ransomed slaves (Alcuin, *Vita S. Willibrordi*, c. 9).

[3] This is the translation given in the *J.T.S.* art. referred to on p. 28, *n.* 1. The original is, " corporale pallium, albis stigmatibus variatum."

[4] Mon. Mog. p. 95.

towel ; [1] (3) to the presbyter Herefrith, incense, and a towel ; [2] (4) to archbishop Egbert, copies of S. Gregory's *Epistles*, a corporal, a towel, two casks of wine (so that, remembering Boniface in his prayers, " he may make a joyful day with his brethren ") ; [3] (5) to abbot Hwaetbert, bed-coverlets ; [4] (6) to King Ethelbald, a hawk, two falcons, two shields, two spears.[5]

To Boniface.

(1) Bugge sends money and an altar-covering ; [6] (2) Eadburga sends books and clothing ; [7] (3) King Ethelbert II. sends a dish, gilt inside, weighing $3\frac{1}{2}$ lbs., also two garments.[8]

From Lullus.

He sends (1) to Eadburga, *inter alia*, a silver graph (style) ; [9] (2) to archbishop Albert, a pall, all of silk ; [10] (3) to abbot Guthbert, *ditto*, also a towel and a cloth.[11]

Denehartus, Lullus, and Burghardus send incense, pepper, and cinnamon to abbess Cuneburga.[12]

To Lullus.

(1) Abbot Guthbert sends twenty knives, also a gown made of seal-skin.[13] Uncertain (owing to the

[1] Mon. Mog. p. 160.　　　　　　　　　　[2] *Ibid.* p. 178.
[3] *Ibid.* pp. 180, 251.　　　[4] *Ibid.* p. 181.　　　　[5] *Ibid.* p. 213.
[6] *Ibid.* p. 75.　　　　　　　　　　　[7] *Ibid.* pp. 98–99, 213.
[8] *Ibid.* p. 255.　　　　　[9] *Ibid.* p. 214.　　　[10] *Ibid.* p. 288.
[11] *Ibid.* pp. 289–290. In *Vita Cutb.* c. 37, we read of a cloth which was sent by an abbess to Cuthbert, and which he laid aside. He intended that it should be used as a cerement for his own body.
[12] Mon. Mog. p. 110.　　　　　[13] *Ibid.* p. 301. Cf. *Vita Cutb.* c. 10.

death of the bearer) if these presents had been delivered, he now sends other presents—two palls (one white, the other coloured) " of very fine workmanship," books, and a bell ; [1] (2) the presbyter Ingalice sends four knives, a silver pencase, and a towel ; [2] (3) bishop Cyneheard sends an assortment of articles of clothing ; [3] (4) archbishop Bregwin sends a receptacle made of bones ; [4] (5) abbot Botwin sends six mantles ; [5] (6) King Alhred and Queen Osgeofu send twelve cloaks and a gold ring.[6]

Alcuin points out the rarity of oil in Britain, and sends some to his master, Colcu.[7] It was to be used by bishops for ecclesiastical purposes.[8]

King Charles sends to King Offa a girdle, a sword, and two silken cloaks.[9] Robes were sent at the same time to the various sees of Mercia.[10] Similar gifts intended for Northumbrian sees were withdrawn, because of Charles's indignation at the murder of King Ethelred.[11]

[1] Mon. Mog. p. 301.   [2] Ibid. p. 216.   [3] Ibid. pp. 270, 287.
[4] Ibid. p. 278.   [5] Ibid. p. 296.   [6] Ibid. p. 285.
[7] Mon. Alc. pp. 167-168. On Colcu, see S.D. p. 33.
[8] Numerous instances of the ecclesiastical use of oil may be found in Egbert's *Pontifical* (Surtees Soc.). It was to be used (1) at the consecration of a bishop (p. 3) ; (2) at the ordination of priests, deacons, etc. (pp. 21, 24) ; (3) at the coronation of a king (p. 101) ; (4) at the consecration of a church (pp. 39, 40, 42, 45, 47) ; (5) at Confirmation. The rubric runs : " Hic debet mittere chrisma in fronte ipsius hominis, et dicere : Accipe signum sanctae cru✝cis chrismate salutis in Christo Jesu in vitam aeternam. Amen." (p. 7.)
[9] Mon. Alc. p. 289.   [10] Ibid. pp. 288-289.   [11] V. sup. p. 5.

CHAPTER VIII

PERSONALIA

SOME of the letters which we have been considering are more or less of an official character—*e.g.* that which contains the report to Pope Adrian I. by the legates George and Theophylact.[1] But others are of a much more personal and intimate character, enabling us to picture the personalities of the writers. We often find autobiographical or biographical details which supplement or corroborate other accounts. There are times when an impression of extraordinary vividness is left upon our minds by the perusal of these letters. This is the case with regard to some of the lesser-known correspondents, as well as with regard to such well-known personages as Bede, Boniface, Lullus, and Alcuin. What could be more vivid than a letter written to Lullus by Guthbert, abbot of Wearmouth and Jarrow?[2] We seem to see the good abbot as he reverently placed the silken covering over the relics of his beloved master, Bede. We seem to see him as, with no less reverence, he placed a covering (intended for his own protection against the cold) over the altar

---

[1] H. & S. iii. 447 ff.   [2] Mon. Mog. pp. 300-302.

in the church of S. Paul. We seem to see his monastic copyists hindered by cold hands in their labour of transcribing the works of Bede. In only a lesser degree, we get a vivid picture of Cyneheard, bishop of Winchester. His letters to Lullus reveal him as a man of deep piety, and as a restless seeker after knowledge.[1] Of a famous predecessor in that see—Daniel—we are also enabled to get a vivid picture, as we read of his failing health and loss of sight, but also of his trust in God.[2] We shall try to gather up from these letters some autobiographical and biographical details which may make more real to us the personalities of Bede, Boniface, Lullus, and Alcuin.

(i) BEDE

In the ordinary sense of the term, we do not find many autobiographical details in Bede's letters. Yet these letters help us, in no small degree, to realise the personality of the writer. They deepen our impression of his piety, his humility, his industry, and his conscientiousness.[3] We shall take these points in order :

(a) *Piety.* He writes with regard to his work on the building of the Temple (allegorical exposition). The letter is addressed to Acca, and concludes with a

[1] Mon. Mog. pp. 268–270, 287.
[2] *Ibid.* p. 166.
[3] For Alcuin's panegyric on Bede, see *De Pontif. Ebor.* 1287 ff.

request for that beloved bishop's prayers.[1] He asks
the prayers of all who may read his exposition of
S. Mark's Gospel.[2] He begs that Nothelm and his
brethren will remember to intercede for his health,
both of body and mind.[3]

(b) *Humility.* He wrote a work dealing with difficulties in the Books of Kings, and concludes a letter to
Nothelm with a characteristic request—" If, con-
cerning those points on which I have written, you
should chance to find anything more suitably explained
anywhere—a thing which could very easily happen—
do not hesitate to send it to me quickly." [4]

(c) *Industry.* A remarkable illustration of his
industry may be found in his obedience to a command
laid upon him by Acca. The nature of this command
is set forth in a letter addressed to that prelate.[5] It
had to do with a work on the opening part of the
Book of Genesis. Several of the Fathers—Basil,
Ambrose, and Augustine—had written on this subject,
but their volumes were too copious and too erudite for
ordinary use. So Acca had enjoined upon Bede the
task of making a selection. The latter did not shrink
from a stupendous task. He selected " as it were
from the most pleasant plains of a wide-flowering
paradise." Not only were the above-mentioned
Fathers consulted, but others were consulted as well,
and the result was seen in his work *In Genesim.*

[1] Migne, *P.L.* xciv. 687. [2] *Ibid.* p. 689.
[3] *Ibid.* p. 687.   [4] *Ibid.* l.c.   [5] *Ibid.* pp. 684-685.

Similarly, in a letter which he wrote to Acca respecting a projected work on S. Mark's Gospel, he expresses his intention to collect what he finds in Patristic authorities.[1]

In writing his commentary on S. Luke's Gospel, he tells us that he was his own *dictator, notarius,* and *librarius.*[2] Here again he made diligent use of the Fathers, some of whom he mentions by name—Ambrose, Augustine, Gregory, and Jerome.[3]

(d) *Conscientiousness.* In his work on S. Luke's Gospel, he wishes to indicate the passages which he has taken from the Fathers, and so he places the first letters of their names on the margin. Then he makes a request that these *signa* would be carefully inserted by any copyists who thought his works worthy of transcription, and that they would follow the example of his own copy in this matter.[4]

In our consideration of the personality of this humble-minded and tireless scholar, one letter calls for special mention, as the personal element comes out very strongly in it, the writer defending himself against a charge of heresy ! We refer to the *Epistola Apologetica,* written to a monk of Hexham named Plegwin.[5] Bede was said to have denied that the Incarnation of our Lord took place in the Sixth Age of the World.[6] This charge was not made by any person in responsible

[1] Migne, *P.L.* p. 688.   [2] *Ibid.* p. 689.   [3] *Ibid.* l.c.
[4] *Ibid.* pp. 689-690.   [5] *Ibid.* pp. 669-675.
[6] Cf. Plummer, *Baedae Op. Hist.* Introd. xli.-xlii., cxlvi.

authority, but by various persons *per pocula*. We can hardly help thinking that he took the matter too seriously. We can almost picture his pained surprise when he heard the news. He was " stricken with horror," he " grew pale." He was especially eager that his defence should be read in the presence of his own bishop, Wilfrid, in whose diocese (Hexham) Wearmouth and Jarrow were situated.

One remaining feature of these letters may be noted, viz. Bede's capacity for forming friendships. He spent a pleasant time at York with Egbert, and it was only illness which prevented a repetition of the visit in the following year.[1] Another pleasant experience—about the circumstances of which we know nothing—was a visit to a presbyter named Wicreda.[2] Both in the letter to Nothelm,[3] and in the letter to Hwaetbert (here called Eusebius),[4] we can see the affectionate relationship subsisting between the writer and the persons addressed. It is, however, in the letters to Acca that Bede's affection finds its most frequent expression. Epithet after epithet is employed, showing the respect and the affection in which that bishop was held. Perhaps the climax is reached when Bede speaks of him as " the most beloved and the most to be longed for of all bishops who dwell upon earth." [5]

[1] *Ep. ad Egb.* § 1.   [2] Migne, *u.s.*, p. 675.
[3] *Ibid.* p. 687.   [4] *Ibid.* pp. 694–697.
[5] *Ibid.* p. 698. Cf. references given above, p. 41, *n.* 1.   Prior Richard emphasises Bede's great affection for Acca (*Hist. Hagust.* i. 14).   The tale (H.E. iv. 14) about the sick boy in the monastery of Selsey was told to Bede by Acca.

(ii) Boniface

Many of the letters written by Boniface to his English friends abound in intimate and personal touches. We can see him wrestling with his own spiritual difficulties. We can see him disheartened at times by the conduct of " false brethren," and perplexed by ecclesiastical questions which arose in the course of his missionary labours. In fact, from these letters alone it would be possible to write a fairly complete biography. But this would be outside the limits of our present inquiry. We shall confine our attention mainly to one or two personal references which show his attitude towards religious life in England, and which tend to exhibit his personality in a clearer light.

Although on pilgrimage in a distant land, he never ceased to interest himself in English affairs. His love of country is shown in a letter which he wrote to the presbyter Herefrith.[1] Deeply grieved at the report of the immoralities of King Ethelbald, he tells Herefrith that the letter of admonition sent to that monarch was due to " the pure friendship of charity," and to the fact that he himself had been born and bred in England. " We are gladdened and rejoice over the good deeds and praise of our nation, but we are troubled and saddened over its sins and reproach."

Boniface, in his English days, had been a notable

[1] Mon. Mog. pp. 177-178.

teacher. His affection for an old pupil is shown in a letter which he wrote to the abbot Duddo.[1] Although, he says, he had been wanting as a learned teacher, yet he had always striven to show special devotion to this pupil, whose prayers and help in study he begs. " Mindful of that devotion, have pity on one who is now an old man, wearied with the storms of the German ocean raging on every side."

Perhaps nowhere shall we get a more vivid idea of the personality of Boniface than from his letter to Cuthbert, archbishop of Canterbury.[2] He there shows a spirit of humility, as he thought of his own unworthiness. He had a deep sense of ministerial responsibility, especially of archiepiscopal responsibility. Nothing could well exceed the solemnity of the thoughts (mainly based upon Ezekiel's warnings) to which he gives expression, as he unbosoms himself to his brother-prelate. It is the picture of a soul in the agony of spiritual conflict. A sense of personal sin and of awful responsibility overpowered him. But it proved an incentive to greater faith. He threw himself more and more on the strength of God. " Let us trust in Him Who has placed the burden upon us. What by ourselves we are not able to bear, let us bear by Him Who is Omnipotent, Who says : ' for My yoke is pleasant, and My burden is light.' " He concludes his treatment of this particularly solemn subject with these words of exhortation to his fellow-prelate :

[1] Mon. Mog. pp. 97–98.   [2] *Ibid.* pp. 200 ff.

" Let us not be dumb dogs, let us not be silent watchmen, let us not be hirelings fleeing from the wolf ; but careful pastors, watching over the flock of Christ, preaching to high and low, rich and poor, the whole counsel of God, to all ranks and ages, so far as God shall give us power, in season and out of season, in the manner laid down by S. Gregory in the *Pastoral Book*."

He showed remarkable perseverance and steadfastness in face of the opposition both of pagans and of " false brethren." Towards the end of his life, he wrote a letter to Pope Stephen III., explaining how the pagans had laid waste and burnt more than thirty churches, and how he had been busy in the task of restoration.[1] He showed gifts of statesmanship.[2] He could work harmoniously with Popes and with Frankish rulers. He could inspire his colleagues with a spirit of loyalty and of affection.[3]

There is something heroic and touching in the picture of the old man sailing down the Rhine on his way to labour once more as a missionary in Frisia.[4] He met death with calm courage.[5] Together with many of his companions,[6] he " passed gloriously and

[1] Mon. Mog. p. 259.

[2] An early instance may be seen from the satisfactory way in which he discharged a mission (the exact nature of which is not specified) on which he had been sent by King Ini and a West-Saxon synod to Brihtwald, archbishop of Canterbury. *Vita Bonf.* c. 4.

[3] A later biographer, Othlonus, tells of English women helpers (Lioba, Tecla, etc.) who came out. Some of them became abbesses. Mon. Mog. pp. 490–491.

[4] *Vita Bonf.* c 8.   [5] *Ibid.* l.c.

[6] Fifty-three, according to S.D. p. 19, and the Continuator of Bede.

happily through the agony of martyrdom to the
eternal rest of the Heavenly Country." [1] These words
of Cuthbert fittingly describe the end of the earthly
career of one who was " faithful unto death."

(iii) LULLUS [2]

We get a glimpse of Lullus in the old days when he
was educated in the monastery at Malmesbury. A
fellow-monk writes to him, reminding him of their
friendship in those days, and recalling the name
Lytel (=Little) which the abbot used in addressing the
future missionary. [3]

Together with Denehartus and Burghardus, Lullus
writes to the abbess Cuneburga. [4] The letter is
especially interesting in its reference to the beginning
of their missionary career on the Continent. After
the death of parents and kinsfolk, they crossed the sea,
and associated themselves with the work of Boniface.

It is evident that Lullus enjoyed the confidence of
Boniface. [5] This may be seen from a letter which the
older man wrote to Pope Zacharias. [6] He commends
his helper, whom he styles his " presbyter," and who

---

[1] Mon. Mog. p. 262.

[2] A very full article (by Dr. Stubbs) on Lullus is in *D.C.B.* iii. 757–761.

[3] Mon. Mog. p. 300.

[4] *Ibid.* pp. 109–111.

[5] It is also evident that he was regarded with affectionate respect
by Albert, archbishop of York. See a letter addressed to him by that
prelate (*ibid.* pp. 290–291), who speaks of his own happiness " in
enjoying the friendship of so great a father."

[6] *Ibid.* pp. 218–220.

was the bearer of the letter, to the Pope's good offices. This bearer was entrusted with messages for the Pope's ear alone—in fact, he was charged with a mission of special responsibility. This confidence may be illustrated by yet another letter.[1] Boniface had been thinking of his own decease, and of the future of his companions. He writes to King Pippin, and bestows a warm commendation upon Lullus. If it were God's will, and if it were pleasing to the king, the writer would like Lullus to be his own successor. He hoped, God willing, that he would make " a faithful preacher and pastor " for the Christian people.

From Lullus's own statement to Albert, archbishop of York, we can see that the writer, in addition to anxiety of mind, was troubled with ill-health.[2] Similarly, writing to Guthbert, abbot of Wearmouth and Jarrow, he says : " I am driven by constant sickness of body to depart from this fleeting light and vale of tears, about to render an account to the righteous and strict Judge. Therefore, as a suppliant, I beseech you that you will pray more earnestly to the Lord for the salvation of my soul." [3] It was more than thirty years after the death of Boniface before Lullus also passed to his everlasting rest.[4]

[1] Mon. Mog. pp. 232-233.
[2] *Ibid.* p. 288. It is in this letter that he alludes, with evident disapproval, to the new legislation of " modern princes."
[3] *Ibid.* p. 289.
[4] William of Malmesbury (G.R. i. 84) quotes some lines, which he remembers hearing in his boyhood, about Lullus. They begin :
" Antistes Lullus, quo non est sanctior ullus."

(iv) ALCUIN

Dümmler, in his Introduction, speaks of the value of Alcuin's letters as a treasury of the Carolingian Age.[1] Several of the letters, he says, "show the spirit of a morose and decrepit old man," but others are of great importance " for investigating the studies and plans of Charles the Great, for perceiving the disturbed and uncertain condition of Britain, and for knowing the friends and disciples of Alcuin." [2] He might have added that some of the letters are also of great value because of the autobiographical details which they contain. In fact, the letters abound with details which help us to picture the personality of the writer. The personal element is very much in evidence in a letter written to Colcu.[3] This letter is of a gossipy character in the news which it contains about the conversion of the Old Saxons and the Frisians,[4] and in its account of the wars of the Slavs, Greeks, Avars (Huns), and Saracens. The writer tells about the state of his own health and the prosperity of Colcu's friends abroad. He tells about the quarrel which had arisen between Charles and Offa, and about the possibility of being sent himself on an embassy

---

[1] Mon. Alc. p. 133.   [2] Ibid. l.c.   [3] Ibid. pp. 166–168.
[4] It is illuminating to read of the methods employed. "The Old Saxons and all the peoples of the Frisians, at the instance of King Charles, some being pressed by rewards, and others by threats, have been converted to the Faith of Christ." On Pippin of Heristal's methods in the days of Willibrord, cf. H.E. v. 10.

to England. He begs his friend's prayers for himself, whether he is sent on this embassy, or whether he remains where he is.

In the course of a letter to Offa, he tells about his own appointment to the charge of the monastery of S. Martin, Tours. This appointment, he says, was not of his own seeking. He begs that orders be given for prayers to be made on his behalf in all the churches of Offa's dominions.[1]

There are many other personal touches in the letters of this great scholar and teacher. A very pleasing trait is the affectionate regard which he felt for the memory of his old master, Albert.[2] An equally pleasing trait is the personal interest which he took in the welfare of his own pupils. This comes out in several passages, notably in the letters which he addressed to Eanbald II.[3]

Even more noticeable than in the case of Boniface, was the interest which Alcuin took in English affairs. Politics, religion, and learning all occupy a large space in his letters. Nor is it surprising that it should have been so. Himself " a son of the holy church of York," [4] he retained his old love of country, even after he had attached himself to King Charles. He gives us an interesting little piece of autobiography when he tells the reasons which caused him to go to that king's realm. Writing to the brethren of the church of York,

[1] Mon. Alc. p. 291.
[2] Ibid. p. 331.
[3] Ibid. pp. 331-339.
[4] Ibid. p. 295.

he says : " It was not from greed of gold—He Who knows my heart is witness—that I came to Francia and remained in it, but for the sake of the Church's need, and for the confirmation of the Catholic Faith." [1] We are explicitly told by his anonymous biographer that he went to Francia " with the authority of his own king and archbishop, but on condition that he should again return to them." [2] He valued his friendship with Charles, and tells us that, by God's grace, the friendship formed with that king had been profitable to very many people.[3] Still, for a considerable time, he entertained the hope of returning one day to his native land. In another letter to the brethren at York, he professes his great love for them. " O, most beloved of all, fathers and brothers, be mindful of me. I shall be yours, whether in life or in death. And perhaps God will have mercy on me, so that he who was nourished by you in infancy will be buried by you in old age." [4] But it was not to be. The murder of King Ethelred, and the generally unsettled state of affairs in Northumbria, caused Alcuin to abandon the intention of returning to his native land.[5]

---

[1] Mon. Alc. p. 255.   [2] *Vita Alch.* c. 6.
[3] Mon. Alc. p. 255. In S.D. p. 33, we read of Charles's generosity to the Church and to the poor, and it is possible that Alcuin may have prompted him in the matter. The story is told in a picturesque form. After the king's victory over the Huns, fifteen wains were filled with gold, silver, and precious silken cloaks. Each wain was drawn by four oxen. The gifts were a thank-offering for victory. Cf. Mon. Alc. pp. 288–289.
[4] Mon. Alc. p. 250.   [5] *Ibid.* pp. 290–291.

EPILOGUE

THE period which we have been considering is marked by sharp contrasts of light and shadow, although perhaps the shadow predominates.

Of some of the Heptarchic kingdoms at this period our knowledge is too scanty to enable us to offer any sort of estimate as to the religious conditions that obtained. Mercia, probably, was the kingdom with the most stable government. Ethelbald, Offa, and Cenwulf were a trio of great kings. On the whole, the Church would seem to have flourished under their rule. The political condition of Northumbria, especially towards the close of the century, was deplorable. That monastic life was disorganised in that kingdom is in no way surprising. The wonder is, not that abuses should have existed in monasteries, but that monastic life should have gone on at all.

Among Northern prelates of this century were several men of outstanding eminence. The Southern prelates are less known to fame. After the death of Brihtwald, there was a fairly long succession of archbishops of Canterbury (six altogether), and some of them had but a short tenure of office.

123

The cause of learning was on the decline. But not altogether. The work of Egbert and Albert, and the fame of the great York school, redeem this century from the reproach of having failed to carry on the traditions associated with Benedict Biscop, Ceolfrid, and Bede.

Of heresy there would seem to have been none. The schism between the British and the English Churches was in process of being healed in some quarters early in the century, and, in other quarters, even more definite steps were taken later.[1]

The interest felt by many persons at home in the missionary work of Boniface is one of the brightest features of the century. The correspondence of that missionary with his English friends affords convincing proof that the spirit of religion at home was animated by the work carried on by Englishmen abroad.

LAUS DEO.

---

[1] H.E. v. 15, 18; H. & S. i. 203–204.

APPENDIX

AUTHORITIES

A. Migne, *Patrologia Latina*, xciv. 655–710.

B. *Monumenta Moguntina* (vol. iii. of Bibliotheca Rerum Germanicarum), pp. 24–315.

C. *Monumenta Alcuiniana* (vol. vi. of Bibliotheca Rerum Germanicarum), pp. 144–897.

Numerous letters, more or less bearing on our subject, are contained in A, B, C. The following are among the most important :

A. Nos. 1–3, 7, 9.

B. Nos. 1, 12, 14–16, 30, 39, 55–56, 59, 61–62, 70, 100, 103, 108, 110, 122–125, 134, 136–137.

C. Nos. 14, 22–24, 27–28, 34–35, 43, 57–58, 72, 79–80, 84–88.

Many letters are printed in Haddan and Stubbs, *Councils and Ecclesiastical Documents*, vol. iii. *passim*. Most of them are contained in A, B, C.

The following alphabetical list may be of interest. It contains the names of many of the Englishmen and English-women to whom or from whom letters were sent. In the fourth column it is shown where these letters can be found. When the references are to A, B, C, the numerals in the fourth column refer, *not* to the paging in these editions, but to the numbers of the letters. The list does not include letters addressed to communities, unless the head of the community is named. Nor is the correspondence included which was carried on by Englishmen abroad with Popes and various persons on the Continent.

Number of letters.	From.	To.	References.
1	Acca (bp. of Hexham)	Bede	Raine, *Hexham*, i. 33.
1	Albert (abp. of York)	Lullus	B. 125.
3	Alcuin	Higbald (bp. of Lindisfarne)	C. 3, 24, 25.
1	,,	Colcu (cf. S.D. p. 33)	C. 14.
1	,,	Beornwin (presbyter)	C. 15.
3	,,	Ethelred (king of Northumbria)	C. 22, 23, 42.
1	,,	Cudrad (presbyter)	C. 26.
2	,,	Ethelheard (abp. of Canterbury)	C. 28, 85.
	,,		
1	,,	Eanbald I. (abp. of York)	C. 36.
2	,,	Offa (king of Mercia)	C. 43, 58.
1	,,	Egferth (king of Mercia)	C. 45.
2	,,	Edilthyda (abbess—formerly queen).	C. 50, 62.
1	,,	Edilburga (abbess of Fladbury)	C. 59.
1	,,	Eardulf (king of Northumbria)	C. 65.
1	,,	Osbald (27 days king of Northumbria)	C. 66.
3	,,	Eanbald II. (abp. of York)	C. 72, 73, 74.
1	,,	Osbert (minister of Offa)	C. 79.
1	,,	Cenwulf (king of Mercia)	C. 80.
1	,,	Ethelbert (bp. of Hexham)	C. 88.
1	,,	Cynebert (bp. of Winchester)	C. 130.
1	Aldhelm	Geruntius=Geraint (king of Damnonia)	B. 1.
1	Alhred (Alcred) and Osgeofu (Osgearn), king and queen of Northumbria	Lullus	B. 119.
1	Bede	Albinus (abbot of SS. Peter & Paul, Canterbury)	A. 1.
1	,,	Egbert (bp.—afts. abp.—of York)	A. 2.
1	,,	Plegwin (monk of Hexham)	A. 3.
8	,,	Acca (bp. of Hexham)	A. 5, 6, 8, 9, 10, 13, 14, 15.
1	,,	Nothelm (presbyter)	A. 7.
1	,,	Eusebius=Hwaetbert	A. 12.
4	Boniface	Eadburga (abbess of S. Mildred, Thanet)	B. 10, 32, 72, 73.
1	,,	Pecthelm (bp. of Whithern)	B. 29.

Number of letters.	From.	To.	References.
1	Boniface	Nothelm (abp. of Canterbury —same person as the Nothelm mentioned above)	B. 30.
1	,,	Duddo (abbot). Cf. Mon. Mog. p. 97, *n.* 1.	B. 31.
1	,,	Daniel (bp. of Winchester)	B. 55.
2	,,	Ethelbald (king of Mercia)	B. 59, 74.
1	,,	Herefrith (presbyter)	B. 60.
2	,,	Egbert (abp. of York)	B. 61, 100.
1	,,	Hwaetbert (abbot of Wearmouth & Jarrow)	B. 62.
1	,,	Cuthbert (abp. of Canterbury)	B. 70.
2	,,	Bugge (abbess)	B. 86, 88.
1	Botwin (abbot of Ripon)	Lullus	B. 129.
1	Bregwin (abp. of Canterbury)	Lullus	B. 113.
1	Brihtwald (abp. of Canterbury)	Forthere (bp. of Sherborne)	B. 7.
1	Bugge (abbess) [1]	Boniface	B. 16.
1	Cenwulf (king of Mercia)	Leo III. (pope)	H. & S. iii. 521.
1	Ceolfrid (abbot of Wearmouth & Jarrow)	Naiton=Nechtan (king of the Picts)	H.E. v. 21.
2	Charles the Great	Offa (king of Mercia)	C. 57, H. & S. iii. 486.
1	,, ,,	Ethelheard (abp. of Canterbury)	H. & S. iii. 487.
1	Cuthbert (abp. of Canterbury)	Lullus	B. 108.
2	Cyneheard (bp. of Winchester)	Lullus	B. 110, 121.
1	Cynewulf (king of West-Saxons)	Lullus	B. 138.
2	Daniel (bp. of Winchester)	Boniface	B. 15, 56.
1	,, ,,	Forthere (bp. of Sherborne)	B. 33.
1	Denehartus, Lullus, Burghardus (missionaries)	Cuneburga (abbess)	B. 41.
1	Eangyth (abbess) & daughter	Boniface	B. 14.

[1] Plummer (*Baedae Op. Hist.* ii. xxxvi.) identifies her with Eadburga, abbess of S. Mildred, Thanet.

Number of letters.	From.	To.	References.
1	Eardulf (bp. of Rochester) & Eardulf (king of Kent)	Lullus	B. 120.
1	Egburg (disciple of Boniface)	Boniface	B. 13.
1	Elfwald (king of East-Angles)	Boniface	B. 71.
1	Ethelbert II. (king of Kent)	Boniface	B. 103.
1	Gregory II. (pope)	Hwaetbert (abbot of Wearmouth & Jarrow)	H.A.A.§ 39.
2	Guthbert (abbot of Wearmouth & Jarrow)	Lullus	B. 124, 134.
1	Hwaetbert (abbot of Wearmouth & Jarrow)	Gregory II. (pope)	H.A.B.§ 19.
1	Leo III. (pope)	Cenwulf (king of Mercia)	C. 84.
1	Lioba (kinswoman of Boniface)	Boniface	B. 23.
1	Lullus	Eadburga (abbess of S. Mildred, Thanet)	B. 75.
1	,,	Dealwin (*magister*)	B. 76.
1	,,	Albert (abp. of York)	B. 122.
1	,,	Guthbert (abbot of Wearmouth & Jarrow)	B. 123.
1	Milred (bp. of Worcester)	Lullus	B. 109.
1	Paul I. (pope)	Egbert (abp. of York) & Eadbert (king of Northumbria)	H. & S. iii. 394.
1	Sigebald (abbot of Chertsey ?). Cf. Mon. Mog. p. 166, *n.* 2.	Boniface	B. 57.
1	Torthelm (bp. of Leicester)	Boniface	B. 101.
1	Unnamed monk of Malmesbury	Lullus	B. 133.
1	Waldhere (bp. of London)	Brihtwald (abp. of Canterbury)	H. & S. iii. 274.
2	Wigbert (presbyter)	Lullus	B. 136, 137.

The above are the main authorities. Some other works, however, will be found useful in connection with a study of these letters.

(i) Special attention may be drawn to Willibald, *Vita S. Bonifatii* (printed in Mon. Mog. pp. 429 ff.). Willibald was a presbyter of Mainz, and wrote his work in obedience to the command of Lullus and another bishop (Cf. Prologue). First of all, he wrote it on waxen tablets, and submitted it to the approval of the two prelates. Afterwards, he committed it to parchment.

It is a valuable work, written within a short time after Boniface's death, and based upon the testimony of persons who had known him (c. 1). The opening chapters (1–4) are of great interest, inasmuch as they tell us about Boniface's early days in England—his home life, his education, his fame as a teacher, his position in the Church, and his relations with Ini, king of the West-Saxons. The later chapters are not so satisfactory, but yet they enable us to understand something of the difficulties with which the missionary had to contend. There is a graphic description of the final scene (c. 8).

(ii) We have a ninth-century anonymous *Vita Alchuini* (printed in Mon. Alc. pp. 3 ff.). The writer bases his narrative upon the authority of Sigulf, a disciple of Alcuin.[1] In the Prologue he says that he will write faithfully the things which he has learned from that most faithful disciple. The first six chapters are an important contribution to our knowledge of Alcuin's early life. The information may not always be absolutely reliable, as where the author states that Bede died a nonagenarian, although the statement is qualified by the remark " as some people say."

(iii) Alcuin's poem *De Pontificibus et Sanctis Ecclesiae Eboracensis* (printed in Mon. Alc. pp. 81 ff., also in Raine, *H.Y.* i. 349 ff.) is so well known as not to need any description. The latter portion especially (vv. 1247 ff.) is o value in what it says about Egbert and Albert. The author

---

[1] Cf. c. 5 for a notice of Sigulf, who is stated to have been a presbyter of York. A close friendship was formed between him and Alcuin.

was here writing about persons whom he knew, and of whose deeds he must often have had first-hand knowledge.

(iv) Symeon of Durham's *Historia Regum* (Surtees Soc.) will be found a useful commentary on the state of affairs in Northumbria.

(v) William of Malmesbury's *Gesta Regum* (ed. Stubbs. R. S.) is of value in connection with political and ecclesiastical affairs generally. The estimates of character which the author gives are of interest. Several times he illustrates his narrative by means of extracts from Alcuin's letters.

(vi) William of Malmesbury's *Gesta Pontificum* (ed. Hamilton. R. S.) contains fuller information on some points than the *Gesta Regum*. This is especially noticeable with regard to Aldhelm. The whole of the fifth Book is devoted to the life, etc., of that scholar. From the Prologue to that Book, it is evident that the writer had a great admiration for Aldhelm, and was not altogether satisfied with the twelfth-century *Life* written by the foreigner Faricius.

Just as in the case of the *Gesta Regum*, we find extracts from Alcuin's letters.

(vii) In connection with the ecclesiastical policy of various kings, reference may be made to charters contained in Kemble, *Codex Diplomaticus Aevi Saxonici*. E. H. S. These charters are of special interest as showing the numerous royal grants of lands and privileges to monasteries. The editor carefully distinguishes between what he considers to be genuine and spurious charters.

(viii) Alcuin's *Vita S. Willibrordi* (printed in Mon. Alc. pp. 39 ff.) [1] was written at the request of Beornrad, archbishop of Sens. The idea was that it should be read publicly to the brethren in church. The work is a vivid

---

[1] The above is the prose *Life*. There is also a metrical *Life* (*ibid.* pp. 64 ff.).

piece of portraiture. It is instructive to compare Willibrord's missionary methods (which certainly were not lacking in vigour) with those of Boniface. When we read about the former missionary's conduct in Heligoland (c. 10) and at Walcheren (c. 14), we may almost say that his zeal outran his discretion. The account of the interview with King Rathbod (c. 11) is of great interest.

In a wider sense, the above *Life* is of value. It tells us something about the beginning of a missionary enterprise which was ultimately to link up, in a wonderful nexus of mutual prayer and of personal service, friends abroad and friends at home. It is true, it was from *Ireland* that Willibrord set out when he began his missionary career. But he was a Northumbrian by birth. Before he went to Ireland, he had been educated at Ripon. We can hardly doubt that many prayers would be offered on his behalf in his old monastery, and that members of the community would, from time to time, join him in the Frisian mission-field.

(ix) H.A.A. This work is printed in Plummer, *Baedae Op. Hist.* i. 388 ff. We do not know the name of the author ; but it is clear, from several passages in the work itself (§§ 1, 5, 10, 40), that he was a member of the community of Wearmouth and Jarrow. The work is a storehouse of information with regard to Ceolfrid.

(x) H.A.B. This work is printed in Plummer, *u.s.* i· 364 ff. It is of great interest and value. There are some passages of remarkable beauty and pathos. We learn much about Benedict Biscop, the saintly founder of Wearmouth and Jarrow. We learn much about his colleagues and his successors. If we read this work in conjunction with H.A.A., we shall get a vivid picture of monastic life in the closing years of the seventh century and in the early years of the eighth century.

(xi) Othlonus, *Vita S. Bonifatii.* This is an eleventh-century work, extracts from which are given in Mon. Mog. pp. 482 ff. The monks of Fulda in that century were not satisfied with Willibald's *Life*. We find abbot Egbert trying to get the Pope, Leo IX., to write a new work. Books were despatched to Rome for the Pope's fuller instruction, and a writer was also despatched. Whatever hope there may have been for the successful prosecution of this plan was destroyed by the Pope's death.

Some ten years later, a new plan was adopted. A literary monk named Othlonus had been enjoying the hospitality of Fulda. Yielding to the requests of his hosts, he drew up a *Life* in two books.

There is a valuable passage in which we are told of helpers, men and women, who came out from England. Boniface, we read, was preaching and baptising in Thuringia and in Hesse. He recognised the need of more labourers " to instruct the great multitude of believers." So he sent for helpers, " and divided among them the burden of his own labour." Among the men who came out, six are mentioned by name—Burghardus, Lullus, Willibolt, Wunnibolt, Witta, Gregorius. Of equally great interest is the list of the women—Chunihilt (the aunt of Lullus), Berthgit, Chunitrud, Tecla, Lioba, Waltpurgis.[1] Of one of these women—Tecla—we read in another work (*Passio S. Bonifatii*) that Boniface " settled her near the river Moin, so that in those places she might shine as a lantern in a dark place, *i.e.* Chizzingun." [2] Othlonus also mentions Tecla's settlement, and he mentions the spheres of labour of other four of the women whose names are in his list.

It is unnecessary to give any description of such a well-known work as Eddius, *Vita Wilfridi Episcopi* (ed. Colgrave.

---

[1] Mon. Mog. p. 490.
[2] *Ibid.* p. 475. Chizzingun=Kitzingen.

Camb. Univ. Press).[1] This work contains many passages which illustrate points in connection with our study of these letters.

Still less is it necessary to give any description of Bede's *Historia Ecclesiastica Gentis Anglorum* (ed. Plummer. Clarendon Press). Here, again, we get much illustrative material (notably in the Fifth Book). There are fairly full accounts of bishops John (cc. 2–6) [2] and of Acca (c. 20).[3] There are shorter notices of Aldhelm, Daniel, and Forthere (c. 18). Specially interesting testimony is given to the learning of Albinus (c. 20) and of Tobias (c. 23).

In view of what we read in c. 7, it is necessary to guard against the danger of over-emphasising the " insularity " of our Church. It is remarkable how many of Bede's contemporaries had, at some time or other, been to Rome. The chapter concludes with a general testimony to the frequency of Roman pilgrimages. Many of our countrymen and countrywomen must have been more or less familiar with Church life in Gaul and in Italy.

We must not leave unnoticed a remarkable passage in which Bede is speaking of political danger inherent in the indiscriminate growth of monasticism.[4] He tells us that, in time of peace, many of the Northumbrians and their sons

---

[1] Eddius's work is also printed in Raine, *H.Y.*, i. 1–103. Eadmer's *Life* (*ibid.* i. 161 ff.) adds little to what we learn from Eddius and from Bede.

[2] In the eleventh century, Folcard, a monk of S. Bertin, Flanders, settled in England. At the request of his patron, Aldred, archbishop of York, he wrote a *Life* of bishop John (Raine, *u.s.*, i. 239 ff.). It is short, but it contains some details, not found in Bede, regarding the bishop's education, his learning, and his work as a teacher.

[3] Acca figures in two twelfth-century works—Prior Richard's History of the church of Hexham, and Aelred of Rievaux's treatise on the saints of that same church—both of which are printed in vol. i. of Raine's *Hexham*. See pp. 31 ff., 184 ff. We do not gain much additional information to what we find in Bede and in S.D.

[4] H.E. v. 23.

were laying down their arms and adopting the monastic life. Good monk as he himself was, he was statesman enough to utter a warning to his countrymen. He ominously remarks : " What will be the end of this thing, a later age will see."

Other points might be mentioned, but the above may suffice to show the great value of this Fifth Book as a means towards a fuller understanding of English religious life in the early part of the eighth century.

In a foot-note on the previous page, reference was made to Prior Richard's *Hist. Hagust.* We saw that this work is of some interest in connection with Acca. It is also of some interest in connection with a later bishop of Hexham—Ethelbert—who is exhorted in a letter addressed by Alcuin to him and " the whole community of those who serve God in the church of S. Andrew." [1] Prior Richard summarises, in a convenient form, some details regarding the life, death, and burial of this bishop. [2]

We have a letter written by Symeon of Durham—*Epistola de Archiepiscopis Ebor.* (printed in S.D. pp. 132–137). So far as information about eighth-century archbishops of York is concerned, this letter does not seem to merit any special attention. It contains, however, some interesting remarks about Bede.

[1] Mon. Alc. pp. 374–375.

[2] *Hist. Hagust.* i. 18. These summary details are also found, but not connectedly, in S.D. pp. 30, 34.

ADDENDA

SUPPLEMENTARY NOTES

(i) Pages 1–9. *Political Instability in Northumbria*

CONSPIRACY, violence, bloodshed, and (towards the close of the century) raids of the Northmen, all help to make up a record of Northumbrian political history in the eighth century. We do not propose to dwell further than has been already done on this gruesome record. We merely give references to the years under which the story is told in Symeon of Durham's *Historia Regum.*[1]

Of course, all the kings were not bad. It is specially said of Elfwald (A.D. 779–788) that he was " pius et justus," and we have a description of his honourable burial in the church of S. Andrew at Hexham.[2]

On the whole, we cannot but contrast the eighth-century kings of Northumbria with some of their great predecessors in the seventh century. Neither in extent of power nor in stability of government do the eighth-century kings compare favourably with Edwin, Oswald, Oswy, and Egfrid, although we must admit that in the doings of some of these great rulers there are things to be deplored.[3]

It is important that we should have as clear an understanding as possible of the eighth-century political situation.

[1] A.D. 732, 737, 750, 758–759, 765, 774, 778–780, 788, 790–794, 796, 798–800.
[2] S.D. pp. 25, 29.
[3] H.E. iii. 14, iv. 26 ; Eddius, cc. 34–39.

It will enable us to form a juster estimate of the religious life of the period, if we see something of the dark background against which the work of the Church had to be carried on.

(ii) Page 23. *English Missionaries and Home Influences*

One of the most hopeful signs of the vitality of English religious life in the eighth century was the interest taken by persons at home in the missionary work on the Continent, and the fact that many of these persons were ready to volunteer for such service. We have noticed the testimony given by Cuthbert, archbishop of Canterbury, both to the numbers and to the character of the recruits in the days of Boniface. There would seem to have been no slackening of zeal in the days of Lullus. One of his helpers, a priest named Wigbert, writes two letters while on a visit to England. If any door were open for missionary work among the Continental Saxons, many people, he states, were eager to hasten to the work.[1] But we must not imagine that the path was always made easy for would-be recruits. Doubtless there was often opposition on the part of kinsfolk. This may be illustrated from the case of Wigbert himself. Pressure was being put upon him to stay in England. His friends and kinsfolk would give him land and inheritance if he would stay permanently with them: otherwise, these possessions would go to strangers.[2] It might almost seem as if Wigbert's own resolution was wavering, although he professes that, if his life is spared, he is ready, God willing, to obey Lullus's commands. The above case may well have been typical of others.[3]

[1] Mon. Mog. p. 304.
[2] *Ibid.* p. 306.
[3] For strong parental opposition (eventually overcome) to the desire of Winfrid (Boniface) for the monastic life, see *Vita Bonf.* c. 1.

(iii) Pages 32–35. *English Pilgrimages to Rome*

The Canterbury pilgrimage, as described by Chaucer, seems to have more or less partaken of the nature of a pleasant outing. It was far different, however, with regard to pilgrimages from England to Rome in the eighth century. Charles, it is true, was willing to grant facilities to pilgrims through the Frankish dominions, and the pilgrims' path was sometimes smoothed by letters of commendation.[1] Nevertheless, it was a toilsome journey. Progress must often have been very slow. Probably Ceolfrid's pilgrimage was an extreme instance.[2] Three times his ship, before reaching Gaul, was driven to land. His great age and weakness made it impossible for him always to ride, and he had to be carried on a horse litter. As it was, more than three months elapsed from the time he left the Humber till he reached Langres. That so many people from England should have been willing to undertake these Roman pilgrimages, with their incidental hardships, speaks much for the reality of their devotion.

(iv) Pages 63, 89, 96. *The Libraries of (a) Wearmouth and Jarrow, (b) Hexham*

(*a*) *Wearmouth and Jarrow.* Alcuin gives us a list of some of the authors to be found in the York library of his day.[3] Bede speaks of the library at Wearmouth and Jarrow in a *general* manner : it was " most noble and most copious, necessary for the instruction of the Church." [4] We are told by the anonymous biographer of the abbots that the library was enlarged by Ceolfrid.[5] He caused three copies of the new translation of the Holy Scriptures (the

---

[1] *V. sup.* pp. 13, 33–34.   [2] H.A.A. §§ 31–33.
[3] *De Pontif. Ebor.* 1535 ff.
[4] H.A.B. § 11. Similarly, S.D. p. 136—" an abundance of books of every kind."   [5] H.A.A. § 20.

Vulgate) to be drawn up.[1] One copy was placed in
the church at Wearmouth, another copy in the church at
Jarrow, " so that it was possible for all who wished to read
any chapter of either Testament to find at hand what
they sought." [2] The third copy he took with him on
his last pilgrimage, intending it as a gift to the Pope
(Gregory II.).[3] This third copy has been identified with
the Codex Amiatinus of the Vulgate.[4]

(b) *Hexham.* Acca collected various " ecclesiastical
volumes " (including Lives of the Saints), placing them
in a " most ample and most noble library " which he
formed at Hexham.[5] With this meagre information we
must be content. Dr. Raine, referring to Acca's letter in
which Bede is urged to undertake an exposition of S. Luke's
Gospel, says : " Acca makes quotations from several
classical authors, and refers to more than one of the Fathers.
Of course, he may have seen these works when he was in
Italy with Wilfrid, but it is much more probable that he
had them in the library at Hexham." [6]

Prior Richard closes the first book of his History with
a mention of the Danish inroad under Haldene in A.D. 875,
and speaks of the widespread destruction by fire and sword.[7]
Aelred of Rievaux tells of the destruction of the church
at Hexham. " Whatever was of wood, the fire destroyed.
That most noble library, which the holy bishop had
founded, entirely perished." [8]

(v) Pages 64–65. *Bede's Description of (a) Ceolfrid, (b)
Hwaetbert*

(a) *Ceolfrid.* Cf. H.A.B. *passim.* Bede was brought into
close personal relationship with Ceolfrid, who was one of

[1] H.A.A. l.c.   [2] *Ibid.* l.c.   [3] *Ibid.* l.c.
[4] Plummer, *Baedae Op. Hist.* Introd. xix.   [5] H.E. v. 20.
[6] Raine, *Hexham,* i. 32, *n.g.*   [7] *Hist. Hagust.* i. 19.
[8] *De Sanctis Hagust.* c. 11.

his teachers, and at whose bidding he was ordained both to the diaconate and to the priesthood.[1] At the time of Benedict Biscop's illness and death, Bede had not yet grown up to manhood, but he was old enough to remember the circumstances under which Ceolfrid was appointed abbot of Wearmouth and Jarrow ("one monastery, although situated in two places"). Doubtless he was an eye-witness of the poignant scene at Wearmouth when Ceolfrid took farewell of the sorrowing monks, crossed the river, and rode off on the first stage of his pilgrimage. Some of the pilgrims—there were more than eighty of them—continued their journey to Rome after their beloved master's death and burial at Langres, some could not for a time tear themselves away from the place where his body rested, and some returned to tell the news to friends at home. From these home-coming pilgrims Bede would hear the story of the final scenes.

(b) *Hwaetbert*. The interesting fact is recorded that Hwaetbert's election as abbot was confirmed by Acca, who gave him the customary blessing.[2]

In Plummer, *Baedae Op. Hist.* ii. 366–367, a passage is quoted from one of Bede's commentaries. There we are told that Hwaetbert's love and zeal for piety had procured for him the name of Eusebius. It is under this name that a letter is addressed to him by Bede.[3] He is also referred to, under the same name, in one of Bede's letters to Acca.[4]

(vi) Pages 74–78. *Requests for Prayer*

We have noticed (p. 77) a very interesting letter in which Boniface asks the prayers of *all* English Christians. We here give the original.[5]

---

[1] H.E. v. 24. [2] H.A.B. § 20.
[3] Migne, *P.L.* xciv. 694–697. [4] *Ibid.* xciv. 692.
[5] Reproduced (by kind permission of the Delegates of the Clarendon Press) from H. & S. iii. 313.

Universis reverentissimis coepiscopis, venerabilibus presbiteratus candidatis gratia, diaconibus, canonicis, clericis, vero gregi Christi praelatis abbatibus seu abbatissis, humillimis et pro Deo subditis monachis, consecratis et Deo devotis virginibus et cunctis consecratis ancillis Christi, immo generaliter omnibus catholicis Deum timentibus, de stirpe et prosapia Anglorum procreatis, ejusdem generis vernaculus, UNIVERSALIS ECCLESIAE LEGATUS GERMANICUS ET SERVUS SEDIS APOSTOLICAE BONIFACIUS, QUI ET WYNFRETHUS, SINE PRAEROGATIVA MERITORUM NOMINATUS ARCHIEPISCOPUS, HUMILLIMAE COMMUNIONIS ET SINCERISSIMAE IN CHRISTO CARITATIS SALUTEM. Fraternitatis vestrae clementiam intimis obsecramus precibus, ut nostrae parvitatis in orationibus vestris memores esse dignemini, ut liberemur a laqueo venantis Satanae et ab inportunis et malis hominibus, et sermo Domini currat et clarificetur, et ut praecibus pietatis vestrae impetrare studeatis : ut Deus et Dominus noster Jesus Christus, Qui vult omnes homines salvos fieri et ad agnitionem Dei venire, convertat ad catholicam fidem corda paganorum Saxonum ; et resipiscant a diabuli laqueis, a quibus capti tenentur, et adgregentur filiis matris ecclesiae. Miseremini illorum, quia et ipsi solent dicere : " De uno sanguine et de uno osse sumus " ; recordantes : quia adpropinquat via universae terrae, et nemo in inferno confitebitur Domino neque mors laudabit Eum ; et adpropinquat via universae terrae. Et scitote : quod in hac prece duorum pontificum Romanae ecclesiae adstipulationem et consensum et benedictionem accepi. Agite nunc de hac obsecratione nostra, ut mercedis vestrae praemia in superna curia angelorum clarescant et crescant. Unitatem et communionem dilectionis vestrae valentem ac proficientem in Christo Creator omnipotens aeternaliter custodiat.

(vii) Page 88. *Ceolfrid's Letter to Naiton*

Ecclesiastical changes made in a Pictish kingdom may

possibly have had little bearing on English religious life. There are two reasons, however, why the above letter calls for special notice. (1) It was the receipt of this letter (from an English abbot) that was the *occasion* of these changes. (2) The letter is of some interest in connection with English learning.

Naiton (Nechtan), king of the Picts, had become convinced that the Roman Easter was the one which ought to be observed. He begged the help of Ceolfrid in the matter, requesting that a letter of exhortation should be sent, by means of which he himself might be able to confute the adversaries. The question of the tonsure was also to be dealt with. The request was granted, and a lengthy letter was despatched.[1] Its learning is undoubted. In its earlier part there is a reference to Plato's famous dictum about kings being philosophers or philosophers being kings. Numerous Scriptural passages are adduced in support of the writer's contentions. We find arithmetical calculations and references to cycles. The familiar contrast between S. Peter and Simon Magus is brought forward in connection with the method of tonsure.

The reading of the letter led to drastic action on Naiton's part. He was overjoyed to find his own views confirmed on the Easter question. He decreed that the Roman Easter should be everywhere observed in his kingdom, and that all his clerics should accept the Roman method of tonsure. The old and erroneous Easter cycles were blotted out, clergy and monks received the coronal tonsure. The Pictish people were brought into what might be called " a new state of discipleship to the most blessed Peter, chief of the Apostles." [2] These innovations, how-

---

[1] H.E. v. 21. Plummer (*Baedae Op. Hist.* ii. 332) says : " Though the letter runs in Ceolfrid's name, there can be little doubt that it is the composition of Bede himself."

[2] H.E. v. 21, *ad fin.*

ever, caused disturbances, and ultimately led to the expulsion of all the Columbite clergy and monks from the Pictish kingdom (A.D. 717).

(viii) Pages 93–94. *Alcuin as Educational Adviser to King Charles*

Alcuin wrote to congratulate King Charles on recovery from illness. It is an interesting letter.[1] There is a notable eulogy of the king. Although the language is that of a courtier, we cannot reasonably doubt that the writer had a genuine admiration for what Charles was trying to do for the promotion of religion and learning in his realm. An account is given of educational work done or projected by the writer himself in his new charge at Tours. His enthusiasm and zeal are apparent. He tells us that he has become all things to all men, so that he may train as many as possible to help the Holy Church of God and to bring honour to Charles's realm. We have already noticed the need which he felt for some of the books he had known in the York library.[2] He does not wish the fruits of wisdom to be shut up, as it were, in a garden at York : he wishes these fruits to be shared at Tours. He himself will do what he can " to sow the seeds of wisdom." The king, on his part, is exhorted to do what *he* can among the young men in the Palace. In short, it is the letter of an enthusiast for the cause of religion and learning. It gives us a picture of an ideal of co-operation between the king and his literary adviser in taking measures which would tend to the attainment of " wisdom."

(ix) Page 97. *Acca's Letter to Bede*

A few particulars may be added to the account given in the text. Acca brushes aside the reasons which caused

---

[1] Mon. Alc. pp. 344–348.　　　[2] *V. sup.* p. 93.

hesitation in undertaking the task. Although S. Ambrose had already written an exposition of S. Luke's Gospel, there was room for another work on the same subject. The ordinary reader could not always follow that Father's line of treatment. " Come now, dearly beloved," he writes, " diligently set about the work in question, expounding the blessed Luke with clear discourse " (*beatum Lucam luculento sermone expone*).[1] Although the writer plays upon the name of the Evangelist, he shows seriousness of purpose. He concludes with a prayer that the God of love and peace would preserve his friend in brotherly fellowship, and would enlighten him to ponder on the wonderful things in the Divine Law.

(x) Page 128. *Boniface (Winfrid) in Wessex*

Willibald does not seem to have known Boniface personally.[2] Nevertheless, in the opening chapters of his biography he has succeeded in giving us a vivid picture of the future missionary's early life in England—of his application to study, of his learning, of his fame as a teacher.

Wessex in those days was peculiarly rich in representatives of learning. Aldhelm then flourished. Daniel and Forthere were learned men. Winbert, the abbot under whom Boniface received part of his training at Nursling, was evidently a diligent student.[3] Ini, the West-Saxon king, seems to have been interested in religion and in learning. Boniface himself worthily upheld the West-Saxon traditions in this respect. It is impossible to read Willibald's biography without recognising, even if allowance be made for exaggeration, that Boniface was no ordinary teacher. His fame was widespread. He had attracted

[1] Bede undertook the task. See his letter entitled *De Evangelio Lucae*. (Migne, *P.L.* xciv. 689–692.)
[2] See Jaffé's remarks, Mon. Mog. p. 423.
[3] *Vita Bonf.* c. 2 ; Mon. Mog. p. 160.

the favourable notice of Ini.[1] In fact, the future missionary was a man who had every prospect of attaining to high office had he chosen to remain in his own land.

(xi) Page 131. *The Monastery of Fulda*

It may be well to explain why the monks of Fulda took such a special interest in Boniface. That missionary, towards the end of his life, wrote a letter to Pope Zacharias.[2] He there speaks of a monastery which he had founded (Fulda), situated in a wooded and solitary spot. It was within convenient reach of the various peoples to whom he had been an evangelist. The monks were men of " strict abstinence, eating no flesh, abstaining from wine and strong drink, content with the labour of their own hands." In this monastery he hoped to rest for a time, and it was there that he wished to be buried.

Pope Zacharias issued a privilege, in which he exempts the monastery from the jurisdiction of any person whatsoever except the Popes.[3]

It was in this monastery that the body of the martyred missionary was ultimately laid to rest.[4]

(xii) Page 132. *Women Helpers of Boniface*

We have a letter addressed by Boniface to Lioba, Tecla, Cynehilda, and their companions.[5] It is of some interest in connection with the writer's humble estimate of himself and of his work. He earnestly asks the prayers of these women, and he concludes with exhortations to steadfastness, perseverance, charity, and patience.

The best-known of all the women helpers is Lioba (Leobgytha). As we have seen (p. 79), she once wrote

---

[1] For the circumstances, see *Vita Bonf*. c. 4.
[2] Mon. Mog. pp. 218–220.   [3] *Ibid*. pp. 228–229.
[4] *Vita Bonf*. c. 8.   [5] Mon. Mog. pp. 239–240.

a letter [1] in which she asks the prayers of Boniface for the soul of her father, deceased eight years ago. In this same letter she alludes to her kinship with Boniface. She also speaks of her mother, Ebba, who was still alive, but suffering grievous bodily infirmity. " I am the only daughter of both my parents ; and would that, although I am unworthy, I may deserve to have thee in place of a brother." She begs that " she may be guarded by the shield of his prayers against the poisoned darts of the hidden enemy."

In *A.O.B.* xxii. 30–34, we get a few more particulars. We are told that Lioba was dedicated in early years by her mother to monastic life under the abbess Tetta at Wimborne. She performed the manual labour which was appointed to her, but her bent was more in the direction of reading and hearing the Word of God. [2]

At a later date she was joyfully received by Boniface as a helper. She was made abbess of Bischoffsheim (in the diocese of Mainz), and we are told of her devotion in that office and of the great influence which she exercised.

---

[1] Written *before* she left England.

[2] As abbess of Bischoffsheim she was devoted to the study of the Old and New Testaments, the Fathers, and the Canons. Except on necessary occasions, she " would never let the sacred volumes out of her hands."

INDEX NOMINUM

INDEX LOCORUM

INDEX RERUM